The Patio
Kitchen
GARDEN

To the memory of Freda Ward
For helping to bring glorious colour to a
black-and-white subject

First published in Great Britain in 2001 by Robson Books,
10 Blenheim Court, Brewery Road, London N7 9NT

A member of the Chrysalis Group plc

Copyright © 2001 Daphne Ledward

The right of Daphne Ledward to be identified as the author of this
work has been asserted by her in accordance with the Copyright,
Designs and Patents Act 1988

British Library Cataloguing in Publication Data
A catalogue record for this title is available from the British Library

ISBN 1 86105 316 9

Printed and bound in Spain by Bookprint, S.L., Barcelona.

The Patio
Kitchen
GARDEN

DAPHNE LEDWARD

ROBSON BOOKS

CONTENTS

ACKNOWLEDGEMENTS

The author's grateful thanks are extended to Mr Fothergill's Seeds, Kentford, Suffolk CB8 7QB, for vegetable and herb seeds and plug plants, seed potatoes, dwarf peaches, Minarette apples and strawberries; Unwins Seeds Ltd, Histon, Cambridge CB4 4LE, for ornamental vegetable seeds; Ferme de Sainte Marthe, Cour Cheverny, France (UK distributor St Marthe PO Box 358, Walton, Surrey KT12 4YX), for unusual and ornamental vegetable and soft fruit seeds; Highfield Nurseries, School Lane, Whitminster, Gloucester GL2 7PL, for fruit trees suitable for growing in containers and trained fruit bushes; Agralan Ltd, The Old Brickyard, Ashton Keynes, Swindon, Wilts, for basket liners and plant protection materials; M.H. Berlyn Co. Ltd, Concorde House, Providence Drive, Lye, West Midlands DY9 8HQ, for Parasene Self-watering Propagators and greenhouse equipment; Creators Econopak, Industrial Estate, Heage Road, Ripley, Derbyshire, DE5 3FH, for the Echo Twin Wall Composter; Haxnicks, Mapperton, Mere, Wiltshire BA12 6LH, for cloches and plant protection products; Hozelock Limited, Haddenham, Bucks, for self-watering equipment; Home and Garden Limited, Enfield, EN1 1SP for Phostrogen in-line feeding equipment.

INTRODUCTION

Spring in the south Lincolnshire countryside. Following last night's heavy rain, the warm, moist air is heavy with the hair-curling fragrance of brassicas. Bold signs erected in fields flanking the main road at the end of our lane proclaim proudly that this crop of cauliflowers is being grown exclusively for one supermarket, the potatoes next door are destined exclusively for another.

I need to make a trip to our local market town, a mere five miles away, but the trip is destined to take up the most of the morning as I join a long procession of cars, juggernauts and ubiquitous white vans following with excruciating slowness the leader of the convoy – a huge, space-age agricultural vehicle resembling a gigantic insect from some distant planet. The flat, hedgeless, headlandless fields around me are full of such alien beasts, busily depositing their insecticidal, fungicidal or herbicidal bodily fluids among the burgeoning, blemishless vegetables, each weedless plant a perfect, scientifically managed copy of its neighbour.

An enormous hoarding on the outskirts of town boasts of the imminence of yet another executive collection of superior properties, all with double garages, showroom kitchens, multiple dream bathrooms, and more top-quality pleats, plaits, frills, valances, pelmets, swags and tiebacks than you can shake a stick at, yet little more garden space than will accommodate the family car collection and a table and six chairs.

Back home again, I turn on the lunch-time news. More speculation, argument and counter-argument on the subject of genetically modified crops. Eggs, beef, pesticide residues – if we eat we may be poisoned and if we don't we will starve.

The obvious solution is to by-pass all food of dubious origin and grow one's own. This is, of course, all very well for those with enough land to devote to home-grown fruit and vegetables. But, surely most of us with modern-sized gardens just don't have the space to be able to sample the vastly superior flavour and texture of freshly picked food?

The encouraging fact is that, although a family is unlikely ever to be self-sufficient in all fruit and vegetables at every time of the year without a traditional kitchen garden, it is quite possible with the careful use of space to produce much of what is required, without increasing the work-load of the contemporary small plot or detracting from the appearance of the space around the home.

Our 17th century cottage, according to the deeds at the turn of the century, was once a property with a sizeable acreage attached to it. By the time it had come into our ownership, virtually all the useful land had been sold off as building plots, leaving it with a garden that is now modest in the extreme. Before we acquired the additional land nearby that enabled me to develop a conventional orchard and vegetable garden, I was faced with the task of satisfying as far as possible my appetite for home-produced vegetables and fruit.

Using the techniques described in the following sections, I found that at certain times of the year I was virtually self-supporting – in fact, sometimes rather too much so, as with the use of a mini lean-to greenhouse 1.8m (6ft) wide and 60cm (2ft) deep I had to sell surplus crops of tomatoes, cucumbers and peppers at the gate to keep up with production!

In recent years, seed breeders have introduced mini-varieties of many vegetables, especially cabbages, cauliflowers, kale and other brassicas, which previously I found difficult to grow in sufficient quantities because of sheer size, and this enables those with minimal space to sample home-grown crops. And with growing bags readily and inexpensively available at virtually every outlet, from the petrol station and hardware store to the corner shop, lack of soil space is no longer a deterrent.

New fruit varieties have made it possible to grow decorative baskets of perpetual-fruiting, pendulous strawberries and full-sized, succulent peaches, nectarines and apricots from miniature trees. Recently introduced dwarfing rootstocks can facilitate a potted orchard of apples, pears, plums and cherries right outside the patio door, while the fact that the heated, double-glazed conservatory is no longer a luxury but an essential feature of the modern home has enabled us to pick oranges, lemons and a whole range of home-raised luxury fruit from the comfort of a wicker chair.

There are very few people who cannot try at least a few home-grown vegetables or fruit. Balcony-raised crops can be just as successful as those grown at ground level, providing some shelter from the wind is given. And even if there is no available space outdoors, fruit and vegetables of a suitable size, such as citrus, tomatoes and peppers, will thrive in a sunny window if the containers are turned towards the light regularly.

There is much to be said for a kitchen garden of restricted size. Weeding is virtually non-existent and regular maintenance minimal. Automation will even take care of watering and feeding if necessary. So with the right techniques, the new millennium gardener can have his or her cake – or rather, fruit and veg – and eat it too.

Daphne Ledward

1

VEGETABLES
The Growing-Bag
Vegetable Garden

This is a way of being able to sample home-grown vegetables without needing any garden at all other than a warm, sunny, paved or gravelled area. It is an easy and productive method of vegetable growing – yields are surprisingly high and quality is excellent if the crops are looked after properly.

Growing bags are not the only containers that can be used for vegetable growing in this way. Almost any tub, trough or similar receptacle that is large enough to be practical will do instead, in which case you would need to fill it with a good, general purpose, soil-less potting compost at the outset. After that, most of the principle is exactly the same.

There are two ways that growing bags (and the like) can be

used for this purpose. One is to devote an entire bag to one particular crop, the other is to grow a wide selection of suitable, compatible vegetables together in the same bag.

THE SINGLE CROP GROWING BAG

If you are especially fond of a few different vegetables – for example, lettuce, peas, runner beans, spring cabbage – this is the method for you. Providing there is enough space for several bags, you may even find that you score over conventional vegetable gardeners. There is less hard work involved, pests and diseases are usually fewer, the growing medium may well be better and crops that are under the eye of the grower are more likely to be well-tended.

Lettuce 'Pluto'

GETTING STARTED

Planting-up can start at about the same time as if you were growing vegetables in garden soil – that is, when the temperature warms up in the spring, usually from March onwards. Choose a good-quality growing bag, usually with a recognisable brand name. Buying cheap ones can often be false economy as the compost may be of inferior quality and the volume less. Thin, limp bags do not generally produce good crops.

In late winter, make a list of all the vegetables you enjoy most. Nearly all vegetables can be cultivated in growing bags. Some will be more cost-effective to you than others, but your choice will be very much a personal matter. If you like spring greens but want to know what they have (or have not) been sprayed with, then by all means have a bag or two of spring cabbage, even though you will get a much higher crop yield from a growing bag of, for instance, runner beans or tomatoes.

Lettuce 'Maserati'

PLANTING A GROWING BAG CROP

Make sure before you start that there are plenty of drainage holes in the base of the growing bag. Some bags are pre-perforated, others have printed indications as to where you should punch holes, but in most cases I find that there are not nearly enough. Growing bag cultivation is thought to be difficult, but this is unfair, as most problems arise from incorrect watering and can easily be prevented at the outset by ensuring good drainage.

Holes should be spaced about 15cm (6in) apart all over the

Cos lettuce
'Bakito'

base; this can be done by punching carefully with a garden fork, but take care that you do not punch right through to the upper surface of the bag.

You will need to cut away the plastic on the top side of the bag to access the compost. If it is to contain a few single plants – for example, tomatoes, cucumbers and peppers – you can cut individual holes, which should be large enough to enable you to insert the plants and water efficiently thereafter, but not so big that the compost escapes or dries out too easily. In general, holes about 15cm (6in) square should be adequate.

I usually make holes by making two diagonal cuts from corner to corner of the area destined for the hole, which then enables the triangular flaps of plastic, still attached to the bag at one side, to be tucked inside around the hole to reinforce the opening and prevent it tearing back further during planting and watering.

If you are sowing your crop direct into the bag, as you will if you are growing, for example, salad greens, peas, beans and root vegetables, then you will have to remove all of the top of the bag except a retaining edge of about 10cm (4in). You can make the big hole in the same way as I recommend for making smaller ones, which again allows you to reinforce the edges of the planting area.

MAINTENANCE FOR BUMPER CROPS

GIVE THE RIGHT AMOUNT OF WATER

Ensure that the compost is damp but not waterlogged when you start planting. In the early stages, another watering will not be needed for some time – how soon will depend on many factors, such as air temperature, natural rainfall, compost texture and the crop itself, so it is not possible to lay down hard and fast rules. Later in the season, however, when the vegetable plants are absorbing a lot of moisture and the temperature is usually much higher, watering at least once a day will be necessary. The compost should then be kept nicely damp at all times since certain crops, particularly tomatoes, may develop physiological disorders brought about by irregular watering.

If you are still unsure when to water a growing bag, there is nothing quite as reliable as your own sense of touch. Insert your finger well down in the compost – if it feels very damp or wet, don't be tempted to add more water, but if it feels dry or just damp, give enough for it just to start running through the drainage holes in the bottom of the bag.

There are all sorts of devices available to help you to water a growing bag, but if you have cut big enough holes around your plants or seed sowing area and you do not allow the bags to become over-dry, it is easy enough to water with a watering can, with or without the rose.

FEED REGULARLY

Growing bag compost contains a basic amount of a quick-release fertiliser to get your crops under way. This is usually exhausted after about 6 weeks and after that time you will need to give a supplementary liquid feed. Extra fertilising is vital from then onwards if you are to get the best possible results. How often depends on the product you are using, but it is usually once or twice a week. Which brand you use largely depends on what you are growing – fruit-producing vegetables, like tomatoes, courgettes, aubergines and peppers, need a potash-rich tomato feed, otherwise any good general-purpose soluble vegetable fertiliser will be adequate.

SUPPORT THE CROP

Some climbing or 'leggy' vegetables, such as peas, beans and tomatoes, will eventually need to be supported. If the growing bag is standing on earth, it is easy to push a long cane through the bag and into the earth until it is firm. The job is more difficult, however, if the bag is standing on a hard surface. Growing bag crop supports are available from garden centres, but possibly the easiest way is to position the bag against a wall or fence to which a piece of trellis, clematis support or pea or bean netting has been attached. The plants can then be loosely tied to it as they grow.

Alternatively, you can stand the growing bag in a wooden trough of the same length and breadth and attach a piece of trellis to the side of the trough.

SUGGESTED VEGETABLES FOR SINGLE-CROP GROWING-BAG CULTURE

SALAD GREENS
('cut-and-come-again' lettuce, endive, rocket, spinach, lamb's lettuce, American cress)
Sow direct in early spring and cut the young leaves when they are large enough. The plants will grow again and should supply leaf

salad greens for the whole season if properly maintained.

ONIONS

Sow thinly *in situ* and use the thinnings like chives. Grow salad onions or pickling types like 'Paris Silverskin'. Sow successionally for a regular supply. Otherwise, grow larger bulbs from sets spaced 8cm (3in) apart.

ROOTS

Sow carrots, beetroot and turnips *in situ*. Choose round or 'finger' carrot varieties and baby beet. Turnips should be fast-maturing varieties or you can grow kohl rabi instead. Use beetroot and turnip thinnings as a green vegetable.

RADISH

Sow thinly, a wide row at a time, with 3–4 weeks between sowings, to prevent a glut.

BRASSICAS

Sow direct, using the thinnings as 'spring greens'. Choose mini-varieties. Brussels sprouts and standard cauliflowers are unsuitable for growing bag cultivation as they need to establish a deep root system. Alternatively, sow mini-brassicas in seed trays and plant out at half the normal spacing when they have produced two true leaves. Remove every other plant when they are large enough to make cooking worthwhile.

LEAF VEGETABLES

Sow perpetual spinach and chard direct and pick regularly without thinning when they are large enough to handle. Otherwise sow in modules, peat pots or similar and plant 15cm (6in) apart in the growing-bag when they are around 5cm (2in) tall.

BEANS
Broad beans
Sow two beans direct, 15cm (6in) apart, and remove the weaker one, or sow individually and plant out 15cm (6in) apart when they are large enough.

Young salads in modules

Dwarf French and runner beans

Sow or plant as above, but after the risk of frost has passed.

Climbing beans

Sow in individual pots in mid-April. Plant out in May when there is no danger of frost. Grow 6 plants to a standard growing bag.

HALF-HARDY VEGETABLES

(tomatoes, cucumbers, courgettes, peppers, aubergines, squashes, morelle de Balbis, korila, Cape gooseberries, tomatillos, etc.)

Sow seed indoors in a light place late February–April. Plant out seedlings into individual pots when they are large enough. Plant outdoors in growing bags in late May–June, three plants per bag (2 plants for cucumbers, courgettes and squashes).

THE ORNAMENTAL VEGETABLE-GARDEN-IN-A-GROWING-BAG

This is a method of growing small quantities of a very large number of vegetables, herbs and edible flowers in a very small space. It is not practical if you want large amounts of any particular vegetables, but it is interesting to do, and does at least provide you with a little bit of something home-grown.

The idea is based on the principle of planting up a container with spring or summer bedding plants, but using vegetable plants instead, arranged not only to provide something to eat but to look attractive as well.

It is possible to grow a dozen or more different vegetables in this way. Choose varieties that are either quick-maturing, so they are picked early and then replaced, or those that can be cropped and will then grow again. Some vegetables – for example, beetroot, chard and carrots – have naturally attractive leaves and should be included if possible for foliage effect. For the best result, you may find it helpful to make a large-scale drawing of the proposed planting before beginning, just as you would with a vegetable plot in the open garden.

Most of the plastic of the upper surface of the growing bag should be removed, as described above for single crops sown direct into the compost. All the plants are sown first into modules, peat pots or small plant pots in early spring and transferred to the bag when they are large enough to assess the visual effect of the individual vegetables in combination with each other.

Varieties with large seeds can be sown singly, otherwise sow a small pinch of seed in each pot and thin the seedlings out to just a few plants per pot when big enough to handle. In the case of vegetables like carrots, turnips, beetroot, radishes and spring onions, each single planting from the original pinch of seed will yield a small bunch of that particular crop.

Positioning the individual vegetables is done in exactly the same way as if you were planting an ornamental container. The tallest are either placed at the back if the growing bag is to be viewed from one side, or in the middle if it can seen from both sides. Low and trailing plants are positioned near the edges so that they will cover what is left of the growing bag plastic. For the best visual appeal, plant two or three of each vegetable or clump of vegetables in different parts of the growing bag.

Keep sowing a regular supply of pot-grown replacements for those crops that are pulled whole, such as radishes, spring onions and mini-turnips. These can then be popped in immediately so the overall effect is not spoilt.

This way of growing vegetables is particularly suited to window boxes and balcony containers. There are all sorts of different combinations that work well and it is great fun to experiment. The following 'recipes', and various combinations of the two, have worked well for me, but the possibilities are almost endless.

RECIPE 1

1   Lettuce 'Bijou': Pick leaves regularly when young for a continuous supply.
2   Salad burnet: Pick young leaves and remove leaflets from stalks. Add to mixed leaf salads.
3   Rocket: Young leaves give a distinctive flavour to salads.
4   Corn salad: Leaves are used in mixed leaf salads.
5   Land cress: Pick young leaves regularly. Use instead of watercress.
6   Salad onion 'North Holland Blood Red' ('Redmate'): Pull when large enough and replace with young plants.
7   Carrot 'Pariska': Pull round roots when large enough and replace with new plants.
8   Beetroot 'Pronto': A few young leaves from each plant can be picked and used, raw or cooked, instead of spinach. After one picking, leave the plants alone to develop baby beets, which will mature later in the season given this treatment.

9   Turnip 'Market Express': These are treated similarly to beetroot. The young leaves make a substitute for spring greens. If the turnips need thinning as they develop, the young roots can be eaten like radishes.

10   Radish, mixed: Replant after pulling.

11   Chard 'Bright Lights': Pick young leaves regularly. Use like spinach.

12   Dwarf French bean 'Saffran' (yellow pods)

13   Nasturtium 'Tom Thumb': Leaves, flowers and seeds can be eaten.

14   Borage: Flowers can be used to decorate drinks and salads. Leaves add cucumber flavour to salad dishes.

15   Calendula: Edible flowers can be used to colour and decorate food.

16   Parsley: Herb used in a wide variety of dishes.

17   Basil, purple: Leaves used to flavour egg, tomato and Mediterranean dishes.

RECIPE 2   Treat and harvest as similar varieties in Recipe 1.

1   Land cress

2   Corn salad

3   Endive 'Très Fine Maraîchère Coquette': Pick leaves regularly like lettuce.

4   Lettuce 'Mixed Salad Bowl'

5   Carrot 'Mokum'

6   Radish 'Sparkler'

7   Turnip F1 'Tokyo Cross'

8   Beetroot 'Albina Vereduna'

9   Spring onion 'White Lisbon'

10   Chard, Rhubarb

11   Dwarf French bean 'Purple Teepee' (purple pods)

12   Nasturtium 'Alaska': Leaves are attractively marbled.

13   Calendula 'Fiesta Gitana': Double flowers produce masses of petals.

14   Basil, Thai: Used in Eastern cookery.

15   Parsley

Edible Hanging Baskets

There are two main types of hanging basket – wire or mesh and solid-sided – though the style varies from manufacturer to manufacturer. Either style can be used for growing vegetables, although the technique and the sorts of vegetable that can be grown in each vary.

The one essential point about growing vegetables in hanging baskets is that, in general, the larger the basket, the more successful the crop. You are unlikely to get a really good yield from a basket less than 40cm (16in) in diameter, as it will not hold enough compost to sustain strong, regular growth throughout the season. Also, hanging baskets need to be attractive as well as functional and the more growth there is, the more attractive they are likely to be. The deeper the basket, the more compost it will hold and the better the root system which will be produced.

The one possible exception to this is the trailing tomato 'Tumbler'. Each individual plant is ornamental enough to be grown as a single specimen although, if you are very fond of tomatoes, you are not likely to be satisfied with the number that one plant produces.

Avoid using self-watering baskets as these can lead to erratic watering – in the early part of the season, they often become waterlogged, and later on they may have dried out completely before you remember to water them again.

WHERE TO HANG

When vegetables are grown in the open ground, they thrive best in an open, sunny situation. Few kinds do well in total or almost full shade and they do not enjoy being overhung by trees and bushes.

This general rule also applies to those cultivated in containers but, in the case of hanging basket crops, which are suspended in mid-air and are therefore under the additional stress of drying out quickly in hot and/or windy weather, the ideal conditions for normal cultivation create problems in themselves.

Constant attention must be paid to watering if the baskets are placed in full sun. The alternative is to choose a position that, although being in full light for several hours, receives some shade, preferably in the hottest part of the day.

It is impossible to say categorically which aspect is best for a vegetable hanging basket, as much depends on the individual site – the proximity of other buildings, high walls and fences, large trees and shrubs and the like. As a guideline, a basket on a south-facing wall will get sun for most of the day, one with an east or south-eastern aspect will become shaded sometime during the afternoon, while that facing west will be in shade until early afternoon. Providing a basket receives about 5–6 hours of morning sun, or 4–5 hours of hotter, afternoon sun during the growing season, most crops suitable for basket cultivation can be grown satisfactorily. The more hours of sun it receives, the more attention it will need. A wall in total shade (usually one facing north) is not usually suitable for a vegetable hanging basket.

PLANTING THE BASKET
THE COMPOST

Always use the best compost available. Vegetables tend to do better overall in a soil-based one, such as John Innes No 1, but this can be a problem with vegetable hanging baskets. Using a soil-based compost makes the basket extremely heavy, even when newly planted, which can put a great strain on the wall bracket, however sturdy. Also, plants grown in this medium are sometimes slower to make growth. While the final product may be better, the objective of having something decorative as well as functional on the wall makes rapid growth in the early part of the season desirable.

Unfortunately, cultivating vegetables in hanging baskets using a basic, general-purpose, soil-less compost is not always successful, especially for crops needing a long growing period. It often becomes 'played out' and tired before the vegetables are ready to be picked, necessitating almost constant watering and increasing doses of liquid fertiliser. This often occurs in conventionally planted baskets before the end of the season but, whereas perfect condition is not absolutely necessary in the case of ornamental baskets, it is vital for good vegetables.

One way round this is to mix half-and-half by volume of John Innes No 1 compost with a good, general purpose, soil-less one. Mixing different types of compost is not usually recommended since it can cause problems with fertiliser imbalance because different composts generally contain a different formulation. However, I find that in this case it can work perfectly well as most of the initial fertiliser is soon washed out through regular, thorough watering. At the time the vegetables are growing most strongly, you will be giving a supplementary feed anyway, so the fertiliser content of any compost will not stay constant for more than a short time.

Specific hanging basket composts are now available, containing additives such as slow-release fertiliser, a wetting agent to facilitate watering and a water-retaining gel to prevent the compost drying out so rapidly. If the weight of the basket is the main consideration, this compost can be used reasonably successfully without mixing it with John Innes No 1. However, the texture is improved if even a little of John Innes is added, although it is not necessary to add as much as 50%.

CHOOSING THE CROP

For the highest yield and the best visual contribution, it is advisable to grow a single crop in each basket. Some plants are more suited to hanging basket cultivation than others. Leaf salad plants and cut-and-come-again leaf vegetables are particularly successful. Dwarf beans have an attractive, semi-prostrate habit that is useful for covering the sides of a basket. One or two trailing, half-hardy kinds look good when hanging on a wall. Root vegetables with pretty foliage that tolerate shallow soil or compost are also worth considering.

Those not recommended are ones that are easily stressed under less-than-perfect growing conditions, such as radishes and spinach, which will quickly run to seed; potatoes, as the growing tubers will work up to the surface of the compost and turn green and inedible; brassicas, which need a deep, rich soil and so are not suitable for shallow containers; and tall, half-hardy vegetables, which would look ungainly in such plantings.

TIP
If space allows, mix ornamental and edible baskets for maximum decorative effect.

Lettuce 'Redina'

Lettuce 'Ritsa'

RECOMMENDED VEGETABLES FOR HANGING BASKETS

LETTUCE

'Lollo Rosso', 'Lollo Biondo', 'Red and Green Salad Bowl', 'Bijou': Can be used to plant up basket sides. Pick a few leaves at a time throughout the summer.

CHICORY

'Fris e Frisela', 'Pain de Sucre', 'Très Fine Maraîchère Coquette': Can be used to plant up basket sides.

SALAD LEAVES

Rocket: starts to flower when stressed but younger leaves still edible; flowers are attractive.

Lamb's lettuce, corn salad, American (land) cress, salad burnet, sorrel: Can be used to plant up basket sides.

Carrots 'Minicor', 'Mokum F1', 'Newmarket F1', 'Pariska', 'Parmex', 'Amini': Sow in March for early summer harvest and sow again in early May. Replace earlier basket with second one after harvesting first crop.

Beetroot 'Albina Vereduna', 'Pronto', 'Modella', 'MacGregor's Favourite': Allow crop to develop over summer and harvest at the end of the season.

LEAF VEGETABLES

Swiss Chard, rhubarb chard, chard 'Bright Lights, perpetual spinach: Can be used to plant up basket sides. Pick a few leaves per plant at a time and allow to grow again.

BEANS

All dwarf French beans and dwarf runner beans are suitable. A mixture of 'Saffran' and 'Purple Queen' is particularly effective as the mauve purple flowers are attractive and the pods are highly ornamental. The dwarf runner bean selection, 'Flamenco', is decorative because of its mix of red, pink-and-white and white flowers.

TOMATOES

'Tumbler F1', 'Brasero'

KORILA

PLANTING UP

Most vegetable hanging baskets are planted up earlier than summer bedding baskets as the plants are usually hardy, with the exception of the few half-hardy types that are suitable for basket cultivation.

The plants establish themselves more quickly and healthily if they are grown in small pots or modules first in a similar way to those used in the ornamental vegetable growing bag. Sow from the middle of March, thin out when they are large enough to handle and plant out when they are well-developed.
Half-hardy vegetable seedlings should be potted on and planted in baskets outside when the danger of frost is over.

If you are using solid-sided baskets, planting is simple as the young plants will form a single layer on the top surface.

Wire baskets can be treated in two ways: either use a solid, preformed liner and plant up in the same way as a solid basket (you will need to choose varieties that will hang down over the edge a little to hide the sides, which do not look particularly attractive), or line the sides with moss or a moss substitute and plant through the sides as well as the top, as if you were using bedding plants.

SOLID BASKETS

Before planting, cover the base of the basket with a 5cm (2in) layer of compost for the plants to root into. Stand the young plants on this and adjust their positions so they are evenly spaced. They can be planted much closer than the recommended spacings on the seed packets, as the method of cultivation is very different. I usually allow a wide enough gap between individual root balls to allow me to work and to firm the compost between the plants easily (i.e. the root balls should touch and should have 2.5–5cm (1–2in) of compost between them).

It is essential that when planted up, the basket is full of either compost or root ball, except for about 2.5cm (1in) of watering space at the top, and there are no air gaps. If you water the compost gently at this stage, it will settle and can then be topped up if necessary. Do not over-water at this stage, as wet compost only dries out slowly at this time of year and the young roots can rot.

WIRE BASKETS

If you are using a preformed liner, the technique is the same as for a solid basket. However, if you prefer to use moss or a moss substitute for lining the basket, the method is different.

First, line the base and the sides of the basket to about halfway up with moss or similar. Use a good, thick layer, which will conserve moisture and prevent the roots overheating later in the season. Add compost up to this point, and insert a ring of plants through the wire sides. If the basket is very large and deep, it may be possible to have two layers of plants around the sides, at about one-third and two-thirds up from the base.

Line the rest of the basket with moss and add a further layer of compost to cover the root balls of those plants that were inserted through the sides and provide a layer for the rest of the plants to root into.

Position the remainder of the plants so that they will eventually cover the top of the basket evenly. Bed in this upper layer and top off with compost, as for a solid-sided basket. Water until it starts to run through the moss around the sides and base of the basket.

AFTERCARE

Leave the baskets in a sunny, sheltered place for a week or so until they have settled down, then hang them in their permanent positions.

Water them carefully for the first few weeks until the plants have started to develop. After that, water more liberally but, if your baskets have drip trays, check that the water does not stand in these for more than an hour or two after watering. If it does, pour it away. Never allow the baskets to dry out as this may cause the plants to run to seed before producing a crop.

Start feeding approximately 4–5 weeks after planting, using a liquid feed specially formulated for vegetable growing. Feed according to manufacturer's instructions, or once or twice a week, until the end of the season.

About 6–8 weeks after the first planting, sow a second crop of quick-maturing vegetables like mini-carrots and baby beet and replace the first crop after harvesting in midsummer.

You are never likely to have a glut to share with your friends if you grow vegetables in this way, but you will certainly have the satisfaction of growing something that both contributes to the ornamental appearance of the garden and tastes good and fresh.

Food from the Window Box

A window box is basically a trough on the wall under the window and therefore it can be used for growing vegetables just like any other container. The two main differences are that window boxes are a generally a feature of the exterior property and therefore have to look good and the crops have to be suitable for growing several feet above the ground.

TYPES OF WINDOW BOX

Window boxes are, in the main, of two different forms. The traditional box is wooden, and is usually fixed to the wall underneath the window by attaching it to two or more strong, metal brackets that are themselves firmly screwed to the wall. It is not usually practical to stand the box on the exterior window sill – it is difficult to attach it safely; it is not usually possible to have a wide enough box to grow anything – edible or ornamental – satisfactorily; the plants will obscure a large amount of light and it will most probably be almost impossible to open the window properly.

The main advantage of this type of box is the fact that it can be constructed to more or less any width, depth and height that you want. The major drawback is that it is a big operation to remove it for emptying, cleaning, treating the wood with a plant-friendly preservative and refilling. It is also not suitable if you want to replace one box immediately with another containing semi-mature plants.

The second form of window box is usually an ordinary plastic trough inside a wooden or metal holder of just the right size to fit the inner container snugly. These holders are often available at garden centres, or you could get them made by a carpenter, blacksmith or metalworker.

The big benefit of this sort of window box is that the inner plastic trough is hygienic, light, and easy to remove for servicing. The minor disadvantage is that you are limited to the plastic troughs commercially available, but there is such a big choice of styles, colours and sizes now that this should not be a serious problem.

As with a wooden window box, this kind should be screwed to the wall very securely underneath the window, not forgetting that you may want to remove the trough holder from time to time for painting or staining.

POSITIONING YOUR BOXES

Any aspect of your house that receives at least half a day's sun in summer (and winter, too, if you want to try your hand at growing winter vegetables in window boxes) is suitable, both at ground floor height and at first floor level and above. However, if the box is higher up the wall, it will be more exposed to the elements and it will be more difficult to provide the adequate and regular watering and feeding that is vital for success.

Do not make life difficult for yourself. You may get far better results from two or three boxes that you can access easily from the path or patio than from several high up on the wall that are a chore to look after. On the other hand, you may have to use the first floor windows if these receive sun and the ones lower down are in shade.

CHOOSING VARIETIES FOR SUCCESS

Because you will want the window box to look good all the time, your choice of vegetables is going to be somewhat more limited than for the growing-bag vegetable garden, although the general principle is the same.

There are various ways you can plant your vegetable window boxes attractively. You can grow one cut-and-come-again crop per box and pick the leaves little and often throughout the growing season. You should be able to use the same sowing all season if you look after the crop properly. As with all vegetables grown in containers, varieties need to be showy as well as tasty to compare favourably with a conventional, ornamental planting. This is the best method if you are not particularly keen on growing a wide range of vegetables, but, for instance, enjoy a fresh, daily salad or the spinach-like taste of some leaf vegetables.

It is possible to have both a summer and a winter crop from the same window box with the right choice of vegetables and varieties. Try mixing several compatible, cut-and-come-again varieties that have interesting leaf forms, in rather the same way as the multi-vegetable growing bag. This will not give you a large quantity of any one crop, but will allow you to sample a wider range of home-grown vegetables.

You can grow one or two crops per box that all mature about the same time and are 'one-off' like carrots or beetroot. If you want continuity of visual interest, the harvested vegetables need to be replaced immediately with something with instant impact. This can be done in either of two ways. If you have the space, you can start preparing a replacement window box while the first crop is still maturing, so once it has been picked or pulled, the old box can be removed and the new one dropped in. With practice, you can get quite clever at growing vegetables in this way and raise a succession of several totally different crops throughout the year from the same spot on the wall.

Alternatively, you can grow replacement plants in modules and the like and replant the existing box. For the best results, you should replace the compost with new, although you will get a reasonable crop if you add about two handfuls of a balanced, quick-release fertiliser such as blood, fish and bone or Growmore before replanting.

A half-hardy crop can be succeeded by an over-wintering vegetable that finishes around the time it is safe to plant out the summer crop, for example, spring greens followed by tomatoes.

Always choose compact, short growing varieties that will not look untidy or straggly when maturing.

RAISING THE PLANTS

Leaf vegetables, salad leaves and mini-root vegetables can be sown *in situ* in spring and, where appropriate, in late summer and early autumn. For instant visual impact, a pinch of seed can also be sown in small plant pots, modules or peat pots and the resulting seedlings thinned out if necessary when about 2.5cm (1in) tall, before planting out in the window boxes when large enough.

Half-hardy vegetables like tomatoes, peppers and dwarf beans should be sown indoors in individual pots in early April, potted-on singly into 8cm (3 in) pots or modules when large enough to handle and kept in a light, frost-free place until late May/early June, after the risk of frost and chilling winds is past.

Pepper 'Apache'

SOME SUCCESSFUL WINDOW BOX VEGETABLES AND COMPATIBLE COMBINATIONS

'Cut-and-come-again' lettuce, e.g. 'Red and Green Salad Bowl', 'Lollo Rosso' and 'Lollo Biondo', 'Bijou', and/or salad leaves like rocket, salad burnet and American (land) cress sown in late March/early April; followed by endive and/or corn salad sown in late July.

Chard 'Bright Lights' or rhubarb chard, sown in late March/early April, followed by kale 'Starbor F1' sown in a seed tray in June and transplanted in August.

Carrot 'Minicor', 'Mokum F1', 'Pariska', 'Parmex' or 'Amini', and/or beetroot 'Pronto' or 'Modella', and/or turnip 'Tokyo Cross F1' or 'Market Express'; sown late March and early July; followed by spring cabbage 'Sparkel F1', sown in July, potted-up singly in August and planted out in the window box late September/October.

Tomato 'Tumbler F1', 'Red Robin' or 'Totem'; or cucumber 'Patiopik'; or pepper 'Redskin F1'; or aubergine 'Black Beauty' or 'Moneymaker F1'; or dwarf runner bean 'Hestia' or 'Flamenco' and/or dwarf French bean 'Purple Teepee' or 'Purple Queen' and/or 'Saffran' and/or 'Ferrari'; followed by leek 'Jolant' sown in seed trays in July, transplanted into deeper trays in late August and planted out late September.

Dwarf runner bean 'Hestia'

PLANTING UP AND AFTERCARE

Make sure there are plenty of drainage holes of a reasonable size in the box. Fill with a good-quality, general purpose, peat-based compost, or, in summer, use hanging basket compost that contains wetting and water-retaining compounds and slow-release fertiliser.

Do not use a hanging basket compost in winter as it may become over-wet. It is not wise to use a soil-based compost, which will become very heavy when damp and supporting a mature crop and can eventually weaken the fixings securing the boxes to the wall.

Ensure that the compost is damp but not saturated. Sow seed *in situ*, if appropriate, or plant out small plants. The tomatoes, peppers, cucumbers and aubergines recommended above should be spaced 30cm (1ft) apart, dwarf beans 15cm (6in), leeks 2.5cm (1in); spring cabbage 5cm (2in) and thinned twice to leave a final distance of 15–20cm (6–8in); lettuce and leaf salad varieties and leaf vegetables (chard, etc) 5cm (2in), root vegetables 2.5cm (1in) and thinned progressively when large enough to eat, kale 20cm (8in).

The fertiliser in the compost will last 4–6 weeks, after which a liquid vegetable fertiliser should be applied once a week at first and twice weekly as the crops mature. Always ensure that the compost remains damp but not waterlogged. Never allow it to become in the least dry. Damp the foliage as well if it begins to look limp in very hot weather.

As mentioned above, it is advisable to replace the compost after every crop. However, it is possible to grow a second, successional or winter crop in compost that was new in the spring if it appears in good heart – not too wet nor too dry and not full of residual roots – when the initial crop is harvested or removed.

A powder or granular, general purpose or specific vegetable fertiliser should be added according to the manufacturer's instructions (which usually works out at around two large handfuls per window box, according to the size) and mixed in very well until it is evenly distributed throughout the compost.

The Two Metres by One Metre Vegetable Garden

This is a way of growing vegetables that I used in the early seventies, when I was working full-time as a landscape gardener and, although I had the space to have a vegetable plot and I enjoyed home-grown food, I simply did not have the time to look after a full-sized kitchen garden properly.

In my case, I took out a rectangle of turf to leave a two metre by one metre (6ft x 3ft) bed in the lawn, but the same principle could be applied to a bed in the patio or even a raised bed, providing it is at least 38cm (15in) deep.

When I originally grew vegetables using this method, it was considerably more difficult to find suitably compact varieties, as it was long before the introduction of 'mini-veg', which can be grown much closer together and still produce good quality, mature specimens. In those days I tended to grow what was available, providing I liked it. I either grew just a small number of each variety, which had a certain novelty value but a very small yield, or I spaced the plants much closer together, and put up with the fact that most of them grew very thin and straggly, although the yield was generally quite acceptable.

Nowadays there is a good choice of suitable varieties for close planting. They are mainly scaled-down versions of larger forms, either ones that are quick-maturing, harvested when young and small and then replanted with another similar crop, or those that can be picked and will grow again. The quantity of vegetables from such a small area is incredible, providing that the scheme is carefully worked out and maintained properly.

GETTING STARTED

The best time to start a mini-plot like this is sometime between September and March, when seed companies are bringing out their autumn catalogues. Make a list of the vegetables you think you might like to grow, then get hold of as many vegetable catalogues as possible and spend some time studying these.

Make a note of the varieties that appeal to you, checking that they are suitable for intensive cultivation and close planting. Most seed companies either indicate which varieties can be classed as mini-vegetables or have a whole section devoted to this kind of crop. Remember that most beds of this sort will be in a fairly noticeable position, so in addition to size and habit, try to find varieties that are also attractive to look at.

Before you place an order, you will need to draw a scale plan. This is important, since it is very difficult to see how the planting will work otherwise. The easiest way is to use squared or graph paper. In the example that follows, I used two sheets of A3 metric graph paper (one for the plot in spring and summer and the other for the same area in autumn and winter) and a rather odd scale in which 30cm represented 2 metres – this fitted nicely onto the sheet and was large enough to be broken down into smaller sections.

THE 2 METRE BY 1 METRE VEGETABLE PLOT

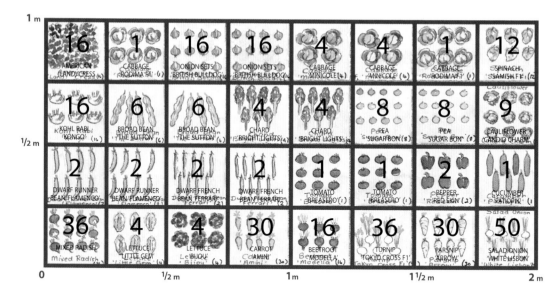

SPRING/SUMMER PLANTING PLAN - indicating the maximum number of each vegetable that should be able thrive in the a vailable space.

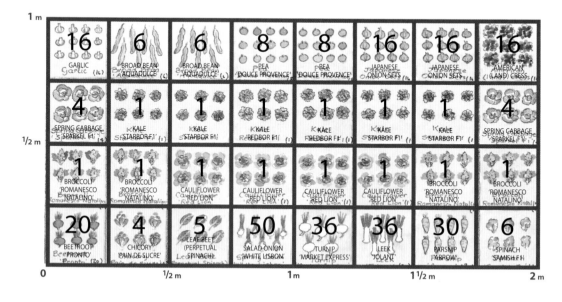

AUTUMN/WINTER PLANTING PLAN - indicating the maximum number of each vegetable that should be able thrive in the a vailable space.

I then divided the 2 metre by 1 metre plot into 32 25cm x 25cm (10in x 10in) squares – a good size for blocks of mini-vegetables. These each measured 3.75cm (1.47in) on my drawing and were large enough to enable me to draw single vegetables or rows to scale if necessary. The individual crops could then be drawn in – some will occupy more than one square to provide a good enough yield.

Where possible, the varieties should be positioned to maximise the good visual appearance of the bed, but what is more important is to make sure that taller plants do not shade shorter ones. For example, if the site you have chosen for your plot faces south and the long side of the bed also faces south, taller vegetables should be placed at the back. If the long side of the bed faces east or west, then it is better to put the taller plants towards the centre, as shown in the example. If your patio faces north, it is not really suitable for vegetable growing at all, particularly if you want to grow crops needing to be sun-ripened, like tomatoes and peppers.

If you intend to use your plot all the year round, you will have to make sure that where appropriate, successional crops will follow on at the correct time. For instance, an autumn/early winter crop of a suitable type of beetroot can be sown without any problem after you have finished with summer radishes and spring cabbages can be planted where you grew kohl rabi in

Radishes

Kohl rabi 'Kongo'

the summer, although you may have to grow them on in larger pots until all of the previous crop has been used. However, you would not be able to grow a winter follow-on crop in the case of, say, leeks or parsnips maturing in December, as by the time you had used them all, it would be too late to start raising anything suitable. In this case, the square occupied by the leeks or parsnips would stay empty until the spring. It is not vital always to have a follow-on crop; in fact resting the piece of ground for a month or two is a very good thing.

Drawing up a timetable of sowing and planting times will make it considerably easier for you to see if you have got your sequences right. If something does not work, the variety or varieties can then be altered before you saddle yourself with seeds you cannot use.

Having decided what vegetables you want to grow and how they are to be laid out, you should send in your seed order or orders as soon as possible, to minimise the chance of some varieties being sold out. It is much better to buy your seeds mail order in this case as you will get a far wider choice and are more likely to find the best varieties. Although the selection in the seed racks in garden centres and other similar outlets is usually good, there is just not the space to include everything, so only the best known and most easily recognised ones are generally available over the counter.

PREPARING THE PLOT

While you are waiting for your seeds, you can start getting the plot ready. If you are making the bed on the patio, you may have to lift slabs or bricks. It is likely that there will be a lot of unsuitable material underneath and this must be removed and replaced with good topsoil (your local garden centre will usually be able to give you the name of a supplier). If the bed is to be raised, the retaining wall will need constructing, not forgetting to leave adequate drainage holes near the base. In a confined space such as this, I find it is usually wiser to fill the raised bed with a good-quality, soil-based, John Innes-type compost. This is more sterile and less likely to cause the kind of problems that can occur in an enclosed situation – troubles with soil texture, the introduction of difficult-to-control pests and diseases, and the like.

If, as I used to, you are going to position the bed in the lawn, the turf will have to be removed and the area beneath dug over thoroughly. One way of doing this and, at the same time, getting rid of unwanted turf is to bury the turf, grass side downward, in the bed, making sure it is at least 1 ft (30cm) down.

Dig in a general fertiliser, such as blood, fish and bone or Growmore, or a dry, specific vegetable food about three weeks before you intend to start planting if you are growing in garden soil. This will not be necessary in the case of John Innes compost in a raised bed, as this contains its own fertiliser.

When spring arrives, everything will be ready to begin. The seed is sown in situ or in pots for later planting out according to type and how they are to be grown, in exactly the same way as with any other method of cultivation. To make it easier to get the crops in the right position, you can divide the bed up into squares as you did with the scale drawing before you start planting, using horizontal canes or wooden pegs and string.

AFTERCARE

You are cropping the land very heavily, so watering and feeding is of paramount importance. A bed at ground level will not dry out as easily as one that is raised, but must still be watched carefully. A liquid vegetable feed should be given from about the beginning of June onwards.

It is not possible to operate a proper crop rotation in such a small space, but wherever possible, you should follow one crop with another with totally different requirements. For example, it is best not to follow cabbages with broccoli, peas with beans, lettuce with more lettuce, and so on.

Tasty Tubs

A couple of decades or so ago, ornamental containers tended to be seen only on formal terraces or balconies and then only in small numbers. Nowadays, no garden, whatever its size, is complete without its cluster of trendy tubs. Until comparatively recently, it was the norm to pack these with bedding plants; later it was realised that other ornamental plants – conifers, shrubs and herbaceous – could be combined together to just as good effect. However, most garden owners still have not realised that many vegetables can be just as striking patio features as the most eye-catching bedding plants, but with the tremendous

Runner beans and edible flowers

35

advantage of producing a delicious and healthy crop as well.

It is no more difficult to look after vegetables in pots than any other plant. Growing vegetables in pots also enables you to produce and experience varieties you are unlikely to buy, even from the most up-market greengrocer or supermarket. Until you have experienced the pleasure of popping a warm, sun-ripened tomato, straight from the plant, into your mouth, you really have not lived!

CHOOSING A TUB

What you grow your vegetables in is mainly a matter of personal choice. Wooden barrels, reconstituted stone, concrete and ceramic containers are all suitable, but 'cheap and cheerful' plastic tubs are just as functional, so the final choice largely rests with how they will fit in with the rest of the garden and how much you are prepared to pay. As the only type of vegetable likely to be outdoors in winter is sprouting broccoli, you do not need particularly substantial containers, although the thicker the sides, the cooler the roots will remain. Remember that terracotta and other forms of unglazed ceramic pots dry out quickly and must be watched carefully, especially in hot and windy weather.

HOW MANY PLANTS?

The number of plants you need will depend on the size of the container and the type of the vegetable you want to grow. As a general rule, small tubs up to about 38cm (15in) will only support one specimen of most types, larger than that and you should be able to accommodate at least three. Leaf vegetables like lettuce

Sweetcorn

Lettuce
'Salad Bowl'

and chard, where most of the whole plant is picked regularly, may be planted closer than, for example, tomatoes or aubergines. Very tall vegetables, such as climbing beans and sweet corn, are really only suitable for the largest tubs. Dwarf bean plants should be spaced about 15–20cm (6–8in) apart.

COMPOST

A good-quality, general purpose, soil-less compost is quite suitable for temporary plantings such as these, although some people prefer to use a mixture of half-and-half by volume soil-less compost and soil-based John Innes No 2, which holds water and nutrients better. You may also mix water-retaining granules in with the compost, which will also reduce watering to a certain extent, but the use of these is not an excuse to neglect regular watering and other general maintenance. If your tubs are on an automatic watering system and you have used water-retaining granules, make sure that the compost does not become over-wet, which can happen early and late in the season and during periods of cool, wet, or dull weather.

PLANTING UP

Check that the tubs have adequate drainage holes and drill more holes if necessary. If you are using soil-less compost, there is no need to have a layer of drainage material, but if there is some soil in the compost, put a thin layer of crushed polystyrene packing blocks in the base of the tub before filling.

Fill the tubs to within a few inches of the rims. Position the young plants, then work compost around the root balls until they are completely covered. The plants should be placed no deeper in the compost in the tub than they were in their small pots. If you have gauged things properly, the tub should now be full to within about 2.5cm (1in) of the top. Water well to settle the compost and top up with more if necessary.

POSITIONING THE TUBS

Vegetables grown in pots and tubs should have a sheltered, sunny spot. You will find that you get the best effect by grouping the pots, rather than positioning them singly or in rows. Mixing tubs of vegetables with others containing bedding or other ornamental plants or fruit is effective, but make sure that plants in one pot do not cast a shadow over those in another, particularly one containing vegetables.

Raise the tubs off the patio an inch or so, using pot feet or bricks, to prevent the drainage holes becoming blocked as the summer progresses.

AFTERCARE

Watering and feeding are the main essentials. The compost should always be kept damp but not soggy. It should never be

allowed to dry out – most troubles with container-grown vegetables are caused through erratic watering – alternating periods of drying out completely and being waterlogged.

It is not possible to lay down hard and fast rules about when to water and how much to give. This all depends on the type of container and compost used, the particular plants grown and their development, and, of course, the time of year – broccoli in winter may only require watering once or twice a month, depending on rainfall, whereas peppers in a medium-sized, terracotta pot in high summer may need watering several times a day!

It is possible to be more categorical about feeding. A good compost will contain enough fertiliser to get the plants established and growing away happily, after which time regular liquid feeding is essential for the maximum yields. Much depends on the fertiliser being used, but, generally speaking, once or twice a week with a liquid or soluble, container plant food or tomato fertiliser should be about right.

SHOWY VEGETABLES FOR TUB CULTIVATION

VEGETABLES TREATED AS HARDY ANNUALS

Sow directly into compost in the tub or sow in pots or modules and plant established specimens out in late spring.

Loose leaf lettuce
Rhubarb chard and Chard 'Bright Lights'
Sprouting broccoli: sow in seed trays, grow on in smaller pots and plant out large plants, one per large pot or tub.

Swiss chard 'Bright Lights'

VEGETABLES TREATED AS HALF-HARDY

Pepper 'Tasty Belle'

Dwarf French and runner beans: sow direct into compost in tub in late spring, or raise plants under glass or on a light windowsill and plant out after risk of frost is past.

Climbing French and runner beans: sow as above and grow up a 'wigwam' structure of canes or string.

Sweet corn: raise plants as for beans. Plant 3–5 well-grown seedlings per tub in early summer to ensure adequate pollination.

Tomatoes, peppers, aubergines; sow seeds under glass or on a light windowsill in late April. Prick out the seedlings singly into small pots when large enough to handle. Plant young plants in tubs outdoors from late May onwards. Alternatively, buy established young plants from a nursery or garden centre in late spring. Most varieties will require tying to canes as they grow. Tomatoes grown as cordons should also have their side shoots removed regularly.

Tomato 'Vanessa F1'

Less common, half-hardy vegetables: morelle de Balbis (right), Cape gooseberry (below right), tomatillos (left): raise young plants as above. These vegetables have a lax habit. They should be provided with canes for support as soon as planted in summer containers and tied in regularly.

Cucumbers, courgettes and squashes: sow seeds (two to a small plastic pot or fibre pot) in a greenhouse, conservatory or on a light windowsill in early April. Remove the weaker seedling in each small pot and pot on into slightly larger ones. Plant out established young specimens in tubs from late May onwards. Allow cucumbers to trail over the side of the container.

Vegetables for Screens

There are a few vegetables that grow tall enough for them to be used as attractive and productive garden screens. We all appreciate the usefulness of 'instant' climbers and tall annuals such as black-eyed Susan, climbing nasturtium, morning glory, sweet pea or sunflowers, yet how many of us would immediately consider plants that would provide us, not only with privacy, but with tasty and versatile vegetables as well?

To be ideal for screening, vegetables need to put on at least 1.2-1.5m (4–5ft) of growth within a comparatively short time and be either capable of standing sturdily without assistance or be suitable for growing up or through a trellis or similar means of support.

FREE-STANDING TALL VEGETABLES

JERUSALEM ARTICHOKES

These may be used as a highly productive substitute for sunflowers. They are perennial, produce a number of substantial shoots very rapidly in late spring, and bloom during late summer, the mini-sunflowers appearing right at the top of the mature stems, which can reach 3m (10ft) or more in a good season. The flowers can be used in for cutting. The plants will tolerate some shade, although the stems may be less stocky and can require some support later in the season. Jerusalem artichokes resemble knobbly salad potatoes, and have a unique, earthy-smoky flavour and a slightly soapy texture. They are a versatile winter root vegetable and can be boiled, baked or made into soup. As with all things in life, there is a catch, this being that they cause the most distressing and unpleasant flatulence in many people, so be warned!

The variety 'Fuseau' is thought to be best for culinary purposes, having the finest flavour and being slightly smoother and therefore easier to prepare for cooking. The dormant tubers are available from most of the larger seed companies in late winter, and should be planted, 15cm (6in) deep and 30cm (1ft) apart in a single row, between January and March, after which time they will start to sprout. The foliage is large and dense, affording good privacy where needed.

The stems continue to grow until late summer and begin to die back in September, when they can be cut down. You can dig the tubers any time during the dormant period and you will find that, even if you think you have removed them all, you have usually left sufficient in the ground to grow again, though to be on the safe side, you may like to replace a few along the row in late winter.

GLOBE ARTICHOKES AND CARDOONS

These are two tall, perennial vegetables belonging to the same family with showy, toothed, grey-green leaves and ball-shaped flowers. Globe artichokes reach about 1.2m (4ft) in height so they are more suitable for architectural screens than functional ones. Fully-grown cardoons are taller, so they can be used where a degree of privacy is required.

Globe artichokes are easily raised from seed sown in the same way as that of half-hardy annual vegetables. They are not entirely hardy, so in colder parts of the country, it is a good idea to grow them on in large plant pots for the first year and then plant them out in their permanent positions the second spring, leaving about 80cm (30in) between individual specimens.

They make a wide, basal rosette of large, ornamental leaves, from the centre of which the flower stalk or stalks sprout during the summer. It is the buds that are eaten as a delicacy, but the plants are worth growing for the ornamental value of the fully open flowers alone. Globe artichokes die down almost completely in winter, leaving only a few central leaves at ground level.

Cardoons *(Cynara cardunculus)* are more difficult to come by, but can sometimes be offered for sale by historical plant nurseries and specialist herb farms. They are planted in the same way as globe artichokes, but it is the stems that are cut into pieces and served as a boiled vegetable.

ASPARAGUS

A small asparagus bed makes a useful division between the patio and the rest of the garden. Being sited near the house, it is a simple matter to gather just what you want when you need it, while the ferny foliage later in the season can be immediately and constantly appreciated from indoors.

Asparagus crowns are usually planted in April, in a trench 20cm (8in) deep. Initially, the roots should be covered with about 8cm (3in) of soil. The trench is gradually filled up over the first summer so that, by the autumn, it is level with the surrounding ground.

Asparagus should not be picked the first year after planting and only sparingly the following season, so that the crowns can build up strength. The ferny foliage of mature crowns may be picked sparingly for flower arranging, but most fern should be left alone or the plants will be weakened. The stems should only be cut down in the autumn when they turn yellow.

Perennial vegetables like these should be given an annual top dressing of a compound balanced fertiliser, such as blood, fish and bone or Growmore, in March. They also appreciate an annual, or twice yearly, mulch of well-made garden compost or well rotted farmyard manure.

SWEET CORN

Sweet corn is a really useful, half hardy, annual vegetable for screening as it grows rapidly, is attractive at all stages and each plant produces several tall, chunky stems that will provide dense cover by the middle of summer.

Sweet corn is best raised indoors and is ideal for fibre pot germination as you will get the best results if the roots are never disturbed at any stage. Sow the seeds (actually the kernels) singly in small, fibre pots in April, either in a greenhouse or cold frame with the lid on, in the conservatory, or on a sunny windowsill. Keep the compost and pot damp all the time. Sweet corn is actually a member of the grass family, and so germinates quickly, producing a two-bladed, grass-like seedling. When the roots are just beginning to penetrate the sides of the pots, pot them on, without disturbing the roots or removing the fibre pot, into slightly larger plastic plant pots and grow on until mid-late May, when they may be planted in their screening positions outdoors.

A healthy sweet corn plant will produce a strong main shoot, with several shorter side shoots at ground level. These will also bear cobs in due course, but most of them will be too small to be of any use. However, the side shoots should not be removed as they help to stabilise the plants.

Most sweet corn varieties will grow to 2m (6ft) or more. To ensure that the cobs are full and succulent, always keep them well watered, and give a weekly liquid feed with a high-nitrogen plant food (such as half-strength liquid lawn fertiliser).

In general, sweet corn plants will produce one full-sized cob and, in good seasons, one or two smaller but still edible ones. To make sure that the cobs are full of kernels, the female flowers must be properly pollinated. The male flowers (tassels) appear before and above the female ones (silks). The tassels produce a large amount of pollen, which in an open garden situation is transferred to the silks by the wind. For this reason, it is usually recommended that sweet corn is planted in blocks rather than rows so the pollen is well distributed to the female flowers. If you are using sweet corn in a single row for screening, you will need to give nature a helping hand by shaking the tassels vigorously to ensure that enough pollen is released to fertilise the silks on the same plant and those on either side. Otherwise, if you rely on the wind, most of the pollen will be blown away and pollination will be incomplete. Inadequate pollination will produce 'gappy' cobs with only a few kernels.

As a further precaution against fertilisation problems, you can position the plants slightly nearer together than the recommended 45cm (18in).

The cobs are ready for harvesting when the silks have turned brown and the sap in the kernels is still running freely but has turned milky. Clear sap indicates that the cobs need a little more ripening time, while if there is no sap at all, you have left it too late and the cobs will be dry, tough and flavourless.

SOME ATTRACTIVE CLIMBING VEGETABLES FOR SCREENING

PEAS

Choose a tall-growing variety, such as 'Alderman', or the mangetout, 'snap' pea, 'Sugar Snap', and provide a support of pea netting on a timber framework for stability and appearance. Sow from late March onward, in drills 2.5cm (1in) deep, and pick the pods regularly when they are young to prolong the cropping season. Water during hot or dry weather, adding a liquid fertiliser once a week.

BEANS

All climbing beans have ornamental flowers, but some are more so than others. Climbing French beans, such as 'Blue Lake', usually have violet-coloured flowers; some, like 'Violet Podded

Screen of runner beans 'Painted Lady'

Stringless', have attractively coloured or marked beans as well (these turn green when cooked, however). 'Painted Lady' is probably the most attractive runner bean, as it produces red and white flowers. It is not a stringless variety, however, and if you prefer these, you can produce a similar effect by growing a white-flowered and a red-flowered variety and growing both up the same support. Try 'White Lady' mixed with 'Lady Di' for a really good appearance and superb crops.

Ideally, runner beans should be sown under glass in small pots in mid- to late April and planted out, usually in late May, when the risk of frost has passed. However, they can also be sown direct into the ground from mid-May onwards, though the plants will start cropping later. You can sow outdoors slightly earlier if you cover the row with cloches. French beans are hardier, and may be sown outdoors from late April.

CUCUMBERS AND MARROWS/COURGETTES

Outdoor cucumbers and trailing types of marrow are usually allowed to ramble over the ground, but the fruits are cleaner and the plants take up much less space if the trailing stems are tied in to a trellis, when you can also appreciate the pleasing, yellow flowers better. The best types for growing in this way are outdoor ridge cucumbers like 'Marketmore' and 'Telegraph Improved'; and marrow varieties 'Long Green Trailing' and 'Long White Trailing'. The marrows will need support as they grow (the feet of ladies' tights, fastened to the trellis, are useful for this). If you do not like marrows, pick the fruits young as courgettes. Most modern courgette varieties have been bred to produce bushy plants, which cannot be trained upwards.

KORILA

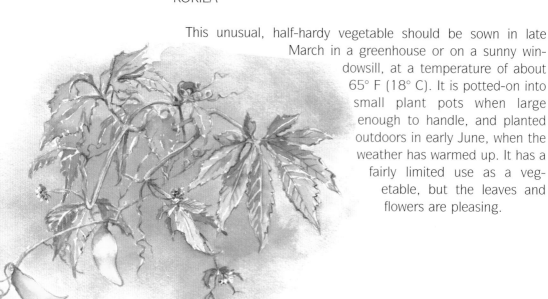

This unusual, half-hardy vegetable should be sown in late March in a greenhouse or on a sunny windowsill, at a temperature of about 65° F (18° C). It is potted-on into small plant pots when large enough to handle, and planted outdoors in early June, when the weather has warmed up. It has a fairly limited use as a vegetable, but the leaves and flowers are pleasing.

A Feast Among the Flowers

VEGETABLES FOR THE ORNAMENTAL BORDER

Although an ornamental border is not usually a feature of the patio, an attractive flower bed is, undeniably, an important element of the garden as a whole and its proximity to the patio or main sitting area can make all the difference to the enjoyment of a paved recreational area and that of the general vista beyond.

Most modern gardens do not have the space to provide dedicated areas for roses, herbaceous plants, shrubs, bedding and the like. To enable the enthusiastic plantsperson to grow as wide a range of subjects as possible, the well-laid mixed border has largely taken the place of rose beds, herbaceous borders, shrubberies and similar areas devoted to the cultivation of plants of a like kind.

While the greater part of the mixed border should contain permanent types of plants, it is always a good idea at the design stage to incorporate gaps amongst the shrubs and perennials to allow you to grow plants of a more transient nature. These may be hardy or half-hardy annuals and bulbs, but, equally effectively, they may also be edible species with an ornamental appearance.

To work best in such a setting, vegetables should have attractive flowers or fruit (or both) or pleasing foliage. Those with pretty leaves should require a long period before harvesting to reduce replanting to a minimum, or, alternatively, benefit from picking regularly to encourage the production of new, young, well-formed foliage.

There are many vegetables that fit neatly into this category and, with careful planning, you should be able to supply yourself with a good mixture of both old favourites and more unusual varieties.

LETTUCE

Use 'cut-and-come-again' varieties, like 'Salad Bowl' and 'Lollo Rosso'. Red-leaved varieties are the most striking, while green forms, especially those with crinkly leaves, combine well with foliage herbaceous plants like *pulmonaria* and hostas.

Scatter the seed in patches to simulate groups of ornamental plants. Thin the seedlings to 10–15cm (4–6in) apart and pick a few leaves off each plant regularly.

CARROTS

Use a maincrop variety like 'Autumn King'. This can be left to mature all summer and then harvested in late autumn, providing green, ferny foliage over a long period. Scatter the seed over patches of soil at least 45cm (18in) in diameter for the most impact, then cover with a thin layer of finely sifted soil. Thin out as necessary, using the thinnings as 'finger carrots' until you reach final spacings of 5–8cm (2–3in). The wider the spacing, the bigger the carrots.

BEETROOT

Treat in a similar way to carrots (see above), but sow the seeds singly, spaced about 1cm (0.5in) apart, and use the thinnings whole as 'baby beet'. The mature roots are harvested in autumn, when they will be of a size large enough for slicing.

RED CABBAGE

Red cabbage has a long maturing period and the bluish-purple foliage is attractive at every stage. Sow the seed in late spring and prick out into small pots when they are large enough. Plant in the border when they are sufficiently well-grown to enable them to cope with the competition of other plants. Unless the border is very large, you will only need one cabbage per planting space. Red cabbage is usually harvested in early to mid winter. If you remove the head and cut a cross in the top of the cut stalk, several smaller heads will be produced which will continue to provide interest until ready for picking in late winter.

Red cabbage
'Radima F1'

SPROUTING BROCCOLI

This makes a large plant, producing purple or white spears according to variety in late winter and spring. Growing from seed and planting is similar to red cabbage (see above); one plant per gap in the border will definitely be enough. One or two healthy plants are usually enough for the needs of most families. In smaller borders, where space is more limited, try a purple-headed cauliflower such as 'Red Lion'.

CURLY KALE

You can spend a small fortune on inedible, ornamental kale plants for winter bedding schemes, only to find that in a warm season they run to seed soon after Christmas. A much better alternative is curly kale, which is raised in the same way as cabbage and planted out in early summer. The plants stand for months before finally producing flower-heads in spring and a few plants will provide enough leaves for the whole winter.

Harvest either by picking individual leaves (not too old, not too young) or by cutting off the whole head before it gets overmature. Kale is cooked in a similar way to cabbage and has a flavour that is much the same as spring greens, but slightly more pronounced. Removing the entire head will encourage the plant to produce a crop of smaller leaves all down the stalks, which can be picked and cooked like spring cabbage when large enough.

CHARD

This makes a most attractive foliage contribution to a border, particularly rhubarb chard, and especially late in the season, when the leaves turn bright red or maroon. It is sown in exactly the same way as beetroot, but should be positioned further back in the border as the leaves grow taller.

BEANS

Broad beans do not have a particularly long season, but the white flowers are pretty in a gentle sort of way and delightfully fragrant, so are worthy of inclusion in a mixed border.

Sow the seeds in peat pots in early spring and plant in groups of five or six when they are large enough. When the spent plants are removed in the second half of summer, the bacteria in the root nodules will have produced a nitrogen-rich soil in that area. This is highly beneficial to leaf vegetables such as cabbage, broccoli and kale, which may be grown on in larger pots and then planted out for winter use and decoration when the gap becomes free.

Dwarf French and dwarf runner beans may be raised in individual, small pots in late spring and planted in groups of 5 or 6 throughout the border in early summer. They also 'fix' nitrogen in the soil so, the following year, use the gaps where runner beans were grown for brassicas and other leaf vegetables.

Broad bean 'Lingo' flowers

Climbing beans may be used in the ornamental border in two ways. Either plant them as a screen at the back (but make sure you have access to pick the beans) or grow them up wigwams of canes or similar bean supports to provide height within the border itself.

ASPARAGUS

Grow in groups of 5 or 6 crowns towards the back of the border. Allow the plants to establish without cropping for a couple of years, then pick the spears until early June, before allowing the 'fern' to grow up.

GLOBE ARTICHOKES AND CARDOONS

Yellow para cress (left)

Red para cress

Raise plants from seed or buy young plants, and plant out individually. Provide 80–100cm (30–36in) diameter planting areas to allow the ornamental, grey-green, toothed leaves to develop fully and not interfere with surrounding plants.

PARA CRESS

The orange or yellow flowers make a useful and unusual addition to a flower border. The leaves are eaten raw in salads and with tomato dishes.

DRAGONHEAD

This is a perennial plant with mauve or purple flowers, so it integrates well with herbaceous border plants. It is possibly used more as a herb than a vegetable and gives an aniseed flavour rather in the same way as fennel. Sow the seed in early spring in trays of compost indoors, at a temperature of around 15–18°C (60–65°F). Prick out the seedlings into individual, small pots when big enough to handle, and pot on into larger pots when the roots have started to grow through the drainage holes in the bottoms of the small plant pots. Dragonhead is best grown on in pots for the first season, then planted out in the ornamental border during the second spring.

ORACHE

This is a 'cottage garden' hardy annual; the seed is sown *in situ* in spring. Once in the border it will always be there as it seeds freely and the attractive plants are likely to pop up everywhere. They are not overbearing, however, and can usually be allowed to grow on where they appear, to good effect.

STRAWBERRY SPINACH

This is another curious, hardy vegetable that is sown in the spring where it is to flower. It is less invasive than its wild relative, fat hen, and the leaves add a pleasant, interesting taste to leaf salads.

TOMATOES

While all tomatoes with long trusses are suitable for mixed border cultivation, varieties grown as bushes (that is, not trained on a single stem by removing the side shoots) blend best with ornamental plants. The most widely available of these are the beefsteak variety 'Dombello', 'Outdoor Girl', 'Red Alert', 'F1 Tornado', 'Roma VF', 'Canary' and 'Tumbler'. Plants are raised indoors under glass (see page 35, Tasty Tubs). Alternatively, in spring many larger garden centres offer a small selection of tomato plants that can be grown outdoors in borders. These should be planted outside in late May or early June when all risk of frost is past.

PEPPERS

Choose a dwarf, bushy, sweet pepper like 'Redskin F1' or a dwarf chilli such as 'F1 Apache 'and plant towards the front of the border. Raise the plants under glass in spring like strawberries (page 106) and plant out in early summer.

COURGETTES AND SQUASHES

If you have a large gap to fill towards the front of the border, try a bush courgette or squash. Not only are the flowers and fruit attractive, but most of the common varieties have bold leaves that are nicely marbled, producing a similar effect to some of the larger leaved herbaceous plants like Rodgersias, Hostas and

Rheums but with the added bonus of producing a useful vegetable crop.

AUBERGINES

Even if the summer is not warm enough to produce ripe fruits, the mauve-blue flowers of the aubergine are enough to allow its inclusion in a mixed bed or border. Grow three in a group, spaced about 30cm (12in) apart for best effect. Because you are only likely to need a very few plants, it may be more economical and successful to buy in the plants from a nursery or plant shop, rather than raise them from seed.

SWEET CORN

The statuesque plants of sweet corn are architectural enough to warrant inclusion in any ornamental border. Their height dictates that they should be planted at the back of the bed and to ensure good pollination you should allow a big enough area to enable a block of at least 6 or 8 plants to be grown. Sow the seeds singly in small plant pots in April and plant out when the weather is warm enough.

Eatable Edgings
DECORATIVE VEGETABLES FOR BORDER EDGINGS

Most of us, at some time or other, like to fill the bare earth around the edge of a bed or border with decorative, temporary plants during the summer months. It is quite customary to have an edging of French marigolds, alyssum and lobelia or Begonia semperflorens, but it is rare to see a similar piece of ground adorned with something just as interesting yet much more useful, even though this is easily achieved by using suitable vegetables as edging plants instead of summer bedding.

Nearly all common summer vegetables can be used in this way if the right varieties are selected, as can be seen from the following examples. Needless to say, vegetables grown like this should receive the same care and attention as if they were cultivated in a conventional kitchen garden. They will need plenty of soil moisture at all times, an initial feed with Growmore or a similar balanced fertiliser 2–3 weeks before sowing and a weekly feed with a proprietary liquid fertiliser throughout the summer.

LETTUCE AND CHICORY

Use 'cut-and-come-again' types of lettuce, particularly those with red or frilled leaves (see Appendix 1). Sow in situ in early April – the same plants should last the whole summer if the leaves are picked regularly. Choose non-blanching varieties of chicory.

SPRING ONIONS

Used as an edging, these give a spiky effect similar to chives. When pulling, remove individual onions evenly along the row so that you do not create wide gaps early on in the season. As the summer progresses, the gaps between plants will naturally get wider, but as the onions are continuing to grow all this time, they will not be noticeable. If you pull the onions when young, you should be able to sow again for a second crop later in the season.

SHALLOTS

These look virtually the same as chives when used for edging. Although the edging will disappear once the shallots are harvested in August, the large amount of useful bulbs you will obtain from such a scheme will make the extra period of bare earth worthwhile.

CARROTS

For the best effect over the longest time, use maincrop varieties, such as 'Flyaway F1' or 'Autumn King'. The thinnings can be used as 'finger carrots' during the summer and the mature roots harvested in autumn. The seed is sown direct into the ground in drills 1cm (0.5in) deep, and should be sown very thinly to prevent the need to thin out in the early stages.

BEETROOT

Most beetroot foliage is attractive, but particularly the ornamental form 'MacGregor's Favourite', which, although producing misshapen, rather ugly roots, has a good flavour and a high yield. Young plants of 'MacGregor's Favourite' are raised like half-hardy bedding plants and planted out when large enough. Otherwise, beetroot should be sown thinly in situ (the seed is large and can be positioned individually in the drill) and thinned out as the roots swell. The tops of the thinnings may be cooked like spinach.

RADISH

These should be sown thinly and picked regularly and evenly when the roots are large enough. As gaps appear, they can be sown again for continuity of cropping. Never allow them to dry out or they will become woody and run to seed.

Radish
'Cherry Belle'

CAULIFLOWER

Most varieties will get too large to use as an edging, but 'Candid Charm F1' is cut when no larger than a tennis ball for the best texture and flavour, so can be planted for an edging which is really different. Sow the seeds in a seed tray first, and plant the seedlings out in their final positions when large enough. 'Mini-Cargill' is a compact cauliflower that is sown and grown on in the

Cauliflower
'Candid Charm'

TIP

Follow an edging
of beans with a
leafy vegetable
that needs large
amounts of nitro-
gen (lettuce or
chard) for a good
crop the next
season. Beans have
beneficial bacteria
in the roots that
'fix' nitrogen in the
soil. When remov-
ing the old bean
plants in the
autumn, do not
pull them up, but
cut them off at soil
level – this will
leave even more
nitrogen in the soil.

same position. The plants are thinned to about 8cm (3in) apart (the thinnings can be used as 'spring greens') and the heads are cut when about the same size as 'Candid Charm'.

CHARD

Where space allows, chard can be planted to provide a semi-perpetual edging over about twelve months. Use a variety with coloured midribs, such as rhubarb chard or 'Bright Lights', and sow the seeds thinly in late March or early April, direct into the ground where the plants are to grow. The seeds are large, so it is quite easy to space them out well. Keep very well watered throughout the summer, to prevent the plants running to seed. Pick the leaves regularly, but do not remove too many from the plants at any time, or they have trouble growing again.

If the plants still look healthy in the autumn, cover the edging with cloches to protect them from the winter weather and they will grow again to provide a final flush of leaves in early spring, before running to seed.

BEANS

Dwarf French and dwarf runner beans make particularly attractive border edgings. For extra visual effect, choose varieties with interesting flowers, like dwarf runner bean 'Flamenco' or 'Hestia', or a mixture of French bean varieties 'Saffran' (yellow pods) and 'Purple Queen' (purple pods).

Either sow the beans in pots in late April and plant out mid-May or sow *in situ* in late May, when the soil is warm enough. French beans may be sown 3–4 weeks earlier than runner beans if the soil temperature has reached 13°C (55°F).

Potted Potatoes

GROWING POTATOES IN POTS, BARRELS AND PLASTIC BAGS

It is quite easy to grow your own potatoes even if you have no garden as such. You can produce an impressive crop in a very limited space on the patio if you plant them in a suitable container.

The simplest way is to use a potato barrel. Plastic, purpose-made potato barrels are available from most garden centres and consist of a slightly raised base with drainage holes and removable sides that you can slide up and down to get at the crop.

The beauty of this device is that you can remove a few potatoes at a time when you want them, leaving the rest undisturbed to grow on. However, I have also used tubs, old dustbins with drainage holes punched in the bottom and even strong, black, plastic bin liners – the principle is exactly the same. The disadvantage of these is that you have to judge carefully when the crop is ready, as it will all be disturbed when you want to start taking potatoes out. As a guideline, you can start to expect potatoes of a reasonable size either when any flowers have started to die (not all potatoes produce flowers, however) or when the stems at the top of the container start to fall over and the bottom leaves turn slightly yellow.

KEYS TO SUCCESS

Always place the container in full sun. Potatoes grown in shade will have thin, leggy tops and a poor yield of tubers.

To get the best results, is essential to have good drainage. If you are using an improvised potato barrel, you must make plenty of holes in the bottom. If the base is not raised, stand the container on pot feet or bricks to raise it above the paving so the drainage holes do not get blocked.

At no time must any light reach the tubers or they will turn green, so you should not use any container that is transparent or translucent.

If you have a conservatory or greenhouse, you can start off your potato barrel in late February or early March, otherwise it is advisable to leave planting until the end of March or beginning of April. A cold spell in early spring can check growth.

To get a really heavy crop, good watering and feeding are vital. The compost should always be damp but not wet, and I usu-

ally feed twice weekly, using a good soluble or liquid fertiliser.

For the earliest crop, choose a first early variety, such as those listed in Appendix 1. However, if you are not in any hurry, this is an ideal way to grow salad potatoes like 'Alex' and 'Pink Fir Apple'. Other maincrop varieties can also be grown in this way but you will have longer to wait.

You may encounter a small snag when obtaining your seed potatoes in that you only need about half a dozen tubers and most garden centres only sell prepacks with far more in them than is necessary. You may be able to persuade them to let you have a few loose ones, otherwise the best idea is to join forces with any friends and neighbours ready to have a go at patio potatoes with you and split a net between you. If you live in the country, and you know a friendly, potato-growing farmer, you could probably scrounge a handful of seed tubers off him. Some seed companies now offer 'trial packs' of popular varieties, which are more economical if you only want small quantities of seed and some horticultural establishments have annual 'potato days' in the spring at which you can obtain advice and buy interesting seed potatoes in small amounts.

STARTING OFF

There is no need to chit the tubers (start them into growth) first, although you will get a slightly earlier crop if you do. Cover the base of the barrel or other container with a 8cm (3in) layer of soil-less compost, then place about 6 or 8 tubers, evenly spaced, on this (smaller containers will require fewer tubers).

Cover the tubers with about 5cm (2in) of compost, then slightly dampen the planting to settle the compost and provide enough moisture to get the tubers growing. When about 8cm (3in) of growth has appeared above the surface, add more compost until just the very tops of the potato stems are showing. Repeat this regularly until the haulms have reached the top of the barrel. If you are using a black plastic bin bag, you will find it easier if you roll the top down to just above the level of the compost when you plant your potatoes. As you top up, you can unroll the top slightly so it is always just above compost level, until you reach the top of the bag. The planting will be more stable if you use a heavy-duty bag or you can use two or three inside each other.

The time between planting and harvesting varies according to variety, from about 13 weeks for first earlies to 20 weeks or more for maincrop kinds. If you are using a proprietary barrel, you can check on their progress by gently sliding up a side panel. If you have used a bin liner, you should be able to feel the tubers if you squeeze the sides gently.

The yield will vary depending on variety but you can expect on average around 2.5kg (6lb). The relative yield of a well cared-for barrel should be somewhat higher than that of potatoes grown in the open ground, because more tubers are produced on the stems as they are gradually earthed up with compost.

POTATOES FOR CHRISTMAS DAY

You can amaze your friends (and save a bit of money, too!) if you serve up your own Christmas new potatoes. Save a few first earlies if you have grown them (or use early shop-bought new potatoes), and plant them in large pots in mid- to late July.

The method is similar to that described above, though it is probably best to use slightly smaller containers at this time of the year. Cover the base with a thin layer of compost, place about 4 or 5 tubers on this and fill up the pots to within about 5cm (2in) of the rim with more compost. Water well and place in a sunny spot on the garden path or patio. Give more water as and when the compost starts to dry out and start liquid feeding once the haulms (tops) have broken through the top of the compost.

About the end of September, move the pots, which should by now be sporting a good growth of green shoots, into a cool, frost-free place, such as an unheated greenhouse, cool conservatory, light shed or garage, or even an unheated spare room indoors, for the rest of the growing period.

If you have got your timing right, your pots should contain a couple of pounds or so each of delicious new potatoes, the size hens' eggs, by mid-December. Quite amazing!

Salads from the Window Sill

We are constantly being reminded that we need five daily portions of fruit and vegetables to keep healthy. There can be times, however, when even the most fertile cook's imagination runs short of ideas for something different – or even something more or less acceptable to those whose natural inclinations only run as far as mushy peas, baked beans and strawberry-flavoured jelly!

However, I find that most vege-phobes can be persuaded to eat small amounts of salads in the guise of 'cress garnish' and I know at least one person who professes never to have consumed a vegetable (other than chips, of course) in his life, yet will eat any amount of Chinese food containing bean sprouts.

Fortunately, it is easy to raise just about as much as you will ever need of these 'living salads' without venturing further than the kitchen, which is good news for flat-dwellers without even a balcony on which to raise plants. The other good news is that the nutritional value of plants is generally at its highest at the point when the seed is just beginning to germinate – another reason for growing sprouting seeds regardless of how much garden space you have for raising home-grown food.

Suitable plants for sprouting include cress, rape, mustard, Mung beans, alfalfa, fenugreek and brassica seeds (cabbage, Brussels sprout, kale, cauliflower, broccoli, turnip, radish). Brassica seeds taste similar to the 'cress' sold growing in small punnets in greengrocers' and supermarkets, which is generally raised from rape seed and is also a brassica.

There are two basic methods you can try.

THE WET-TISSUE METHOD

All the above salad sprouts can be grown in this way. Use a small seed tray, cress punnet or similar shallow container (preferably with drainage holes in the bottom). Cover the base with a few layers of kitchen paper, paper handkerchiefs, blotting paper, toilet tissue or cotton wool, or about 1–2cm (0.5–0.75in) general purpose potting compost. Add water until the paper or compost is damp.

NOTE

Mung beans are
treated slightly
differently. The
seed should be
soaked in tepid
water for 24 hours
before sowing, or
it may not
germinate. To keep
the shoots white,
tender and juicy,
they should be
grown in complete
darkness from
sowing to cutting.

To dampen the seed. Press the seed into the surface of the compost very gently.

Cover with a couple of sheets of newspaper, and place in a
warm, dark place until the seed starts to sprout. The seed packets
generally recommend using the airing cupboard for germination,
but I find ours is too warm and tends to dry out the seed and compost too quickly, so I prefer to use the cupboard over the built-in
refrigerator, which is always pleasantly warm but not too hot.

Once the seeds have started to sprout – usually within about
24 hours – they can be moved to a cooler, light spot, such as a
windowsill, to continue. They will be ready for eating when about
5cm (2in) tall. This will take around 5–7 days, depending on the
temperature of the room.

If you like a traditional 'mustard and cress' mixture, you
should sow the mustard seed, in the same container, 4 days after
the cress. Otherwise use the variety 'Polycress', which is a blend
of mustard seed and a new variety of cress that mature at the
same time.

To prevent sprouts surplus to immediate requirements growing too tall and becoming strong-flavoured or tough, they can be
stored for up to 4 days in the salad drawer of the refrigerator.

THE GLASS-JAR METHOD

Place a tablespoonful of seed in the bottom of a screw-topped glass
jam jar and add water until the jar is about two-thirds full. Screw
the top on tightly. Shake vigorously for two minutes, then drain off
the water and repeat twice more. This removes the natural growth
inhibitor coating the seeds that Nature has provided them with so
they only start to sprout when conditions are right. If the seeds are
not adequately rinsed, they will not sprout properly.

Remove the screw top and replace with muslin or a folded
sheet of kitchen roll held in place with a rubber band. Place the jar
in a warm, dark place as before until the seeds start to sprout,
then remove to a cooler, light position. For the whole of the growing period, the seeds should be thoroughly rinsed twice a day.
Failure to do this will encourage the growth of fungus or bacteria;
the sprouts will start to smell fusty or bad and will be unfit to eat.

Germination under these conditions generally takes just under a
day. A tablespoon of seed in a 1kg (2lb) jam jar will fill the jar with
sprouts in 5–8 days depending on temperature. At this stage, they
will be ready to eat. Surplus shoots may be stored for several days
in the bottom of the refrigerator if loosely packed in a polythene bag.

Only certain types of seed are suitable for this way of producing salad sprouts. Alfalfa and fenugreek work best. Mung beans can also be grown in a jar but must be kept in the dark throughout the growing period. Bean sprouts raised like this will have roots attached when removed from the jar, unlike those grown on tissue or compost, which root into the growing medium and therefore have to be cut to gather them. The roots of jar-raised bean sprouts are usually tender enough to eat with the rest of the shoots or they may be clipped off before use.

Do not attempt to grow cress by this method. If you add water to cress seed, it produces a slimy, jelly-like substance and suddenly you have something more akin to a jar of tadpoles. It is impossible to wash and drain the seed, which becomes stuck together in a viscous mess and does not germinate satisfactorily.

The Square Metre Salad Garden

It may surprise you to learn that it is possible to grow much of the salad you will need for a whole summer in an area no bigger than a metre square. The idea is similar to that of the Growing Bag Vegetable Garden. In this case, you can either use a square metre of open garden if suitable, a similar area within the paving of the patio, or a low raised bed. The results should be equally successful and will also provide a useful ornamental feature if you choose the right varieties.

The salad leaves are picked on a 'cut-and-come-again' basis, while the roots, with the exception of radishes, are harvested later in the season after first providing a crop of leaf vegetables for hot or cold use.

PREPARING THE GROUND

The site for the metre-square salad garden must be in an open position, away from overhanging branches and in full, or nearly full, sunlight. You need a well-textured, fertile, water-retentive soil to get the best out of an intensive cropping scheme such as this. If you are planting in open ground, break the area up well to a depth of around 30cm (1ft) and dig in plenty of well-made garden compost, farmyard manure or, if these are not available, the

The square metre salad garden

compost out of old growing bags or similar. If the soil is at all heavy, it should be opened up by digging in horticultural sharp sand as well, until the texture looks more open and it is easily worked with a fork or spade.

If the soil has not been cropped previously, the nutrient level is likely to be quite high, but to ensure that the salads will have plenty to get their teeth into, you can give a top dressing of a quick-release, compound fertiliser, such as blood, fish and bone, about two weeks before sowing or planting.

You can make a bed in an existing patio by taking up a square of paving – if your patio is paved with 45cm (18in) square slabs, you will need to remove four. Remove all the sand, rubble and subsoil in the square to a depth of 30cm (1ft) and replace it with John Innes No 1 compost or good topsoil mixed with plenty of well-rotted organic material.

A raised bed needs to be about 30cm (1ft) in height. If you do not want to commit yourself to a permanent structure, try out the idea for a season or two by laying the bricks or blocks dry on top of the paving to form a temporary, square, raised bed with 1-metre-long sides, which may be filled with any good, general purpose, soil-less compost. The whole feature can be easily removed without trace if you want to move it in the future, or grow your salad crops elsewhere.

Whether or not the bed walls are mortared, you will need to leave gaps between some of the bricks or blocks in the first course to allow the compost to drain. Your crops will not thrive in waterlogged conditions.

SALAD VARIETIES FOR CLOSE CROPPING

Loose-leaf lettuce, which can be picked a little at a time.
Other salad leaves, e.g. chicory, rocket (pick regularly to prevent the plants running to seed); lamb's lettuce (corn salad), American land cress
Radishes
Spring onions
Carrots (baby, 'finger' and round-rooted)
Mini-beetroot
Turnip
Baby spinach

RAISING THE CROPS

You can either sow directly into the ground or raise plug plants first. Direct sowing is easier, quicker and cuts out one stage of production. On the other hand, plug or pot-grown plants can be planted out at their final spacings, need no thinning and make an immediate visual impact.

DIRECT SOWING

For early crops, start at the beginning of March by covering the metre of soil or compost with black polythene, a cloche or bell jars, to warm up the soil. Sow in mid- or late March, or when the soil temperature has reached 12°C (55°F). You can check this with a soil thermometer if you are not sure. Otherwise, wait until early- to mid-April, when the soil has warmed up naturally.

Draw shallow drills, about1cm (0.5in) deep and 12.5cm (5in) apart, with a cane. If you position your first and last crops near the edges of the bed, you will be able to get in 8 rows – unless you have sited your mini-salad garden in grass, it will not matter if the foliage overhangs the bed edges. Water the bottoms of the drills gently but thoroughly.

Sow the seed thinly along each drill, then cover with soil or compost. There is no need to water the whole area at this point. The seed will germinate in the moisture at the bottom of the drill, which will remain damp much longer this way as capillary action has been circumvented.

When the seed has germinated and the seedlings are just large enough to handle, thin out to about 2.5cm (1in) apart (spring onion thinnings can be chopped finely with sharp scissors and used in the same way as chives) and allow the plants to develop until they can be cropped.

THE ONE METRE SQUARE SALAD GARDEN

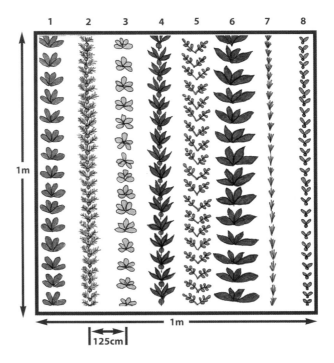

1 Lettuce 'Bijou'
2 Carrot 'Parmex'
3 Lambs lettuce
4 Beetroot 'Pronto'

5 American land cress
6 Spinach 'Samish' F.1.
7 Spring Onion 'White Lisbon'
8 Mixed Radish

RAISING PLANTS IN MODULES

Sow a small pinch of seed in each module or pot in early March. Give some protection e.g. a cloche, cold frame, unheated greenhouse or cool, light room indoors. Thin out to 2 or 3 plants per module when large enough to handle. Once they have recovered from this treatment, they may be placed outdoors in a sheltered, sunny position (check the compost periodically to make sure it does not dry out).

The plants should be ready in April, when the tops are well developed. Remove carefully from the modules (unless you are using fibre pots, in which case, plant the whole thing) and plant in rows, spaced just over 2.5cm (1in) apart, as described above. If, during the course of the summer, the plants appear to be suffering from overcrowding, despite regular picking, every other plant may be removed to give the remaining ones more space.

CROPPING FOR QUANTITY AND QUALITY

LETTUCE AND OTHER SALAD LEAVES

Pick individual leaves, little and often, from all plants equally, when of a size suitable for use in salads and soups or as garnish. Leave the centres of each plant to produce more young leaves.

SPINACH

Treat as above if eating raw. For a cooked vegetable, allow the leaves to grow slightly bigger and remove all but the small, young ones in the centre of every plant. Let the plants recover and bear a second good crop of new leaves before picking again, then only gather in moderation for a while to allow the crop to regain strength.

RADISHES

Pull roots when large enough. Sow more seed in the gaps immediately for succession.

SPRING ONIONS

Pull a few plants at a time and use immediately.

CARROTS

Start harvesting when about 2.5cm (1in) in diameter.

TURNIPS

Pick leaves from young plants and use as 'spring greens' or shred finely and add to green salads for a spicy flavour, but do not defoliate entirely. Let the plants grow again. They will then form roots that can be pulled when about 2.5cm (1in) and used raw like radishes in salads. Otherwise allow them to grow larger and pull for use as a cooked root vegetable when as big as golfballs.

BEETROOT

Treat in the same way as turnips. Use the first flush of leaves as a spinach substitute, then let the plants grow again and develop roots for eating cooked or pickling after they have reached the size of ping-pong balls.

KEEPING THINGS MOVING

Such an intensive regime will soon run into problems if not well cared for. After germination, the plants should never be allowed to dry out and, once picking starts, a weekly liquid feed must be given in addition to the fertiliser applied before sowing. These kinds of plant quickly run to seed if stressed – stress can occur if they dry out, even if only briefly, or when soil nutrient levels start to run low.

AT THE END OF THE SEASON

You can prolong the season by covering the bed with a cloche, but eventually most crops will die off or become used up. Remove all dead, dying and unproductive plants, so the plot progressively becomes vacant. Do not replant (the exception is radishes, which are sown little and often throughout the season).

American land cress is hardy, so will remain green throughout the winter and can be picked regularly. Pull up at the end of February to empty the square completely. It can then be dug over and rested for a month or so.

About a fortnight before sowing again, dig in a general purpose fertiliser such as blood, fish and bone or Growmore. If you incorporated plenty of organic material the previous spring, you may find this will suffice for a second season before adding more. It is not possible to practice genuine crop rotation in such a small area, but it is advisable to plant different vegetables in any particular row from one year to the next. For example, if you had turnips there one summer, you should aim to plant something unrelated, like lamb's lettuce, the next.

If you are growing in soil-less compost in a raised bed, you should replace the compost every spring. In this case, it does not matter if your current year's crops come in exactly the same places as the previous summer's.

With beds in the open ground, it is a good thing to give the soil a year's rest after about three seasons, by growing something completely different, such as bedding plants. If you do not, you may start to experience problems such as disease and reduced yields.

2

HERBS
The Herb Pot

A herb pot is a great way of getting a lot of herbs into a very small space. Herb pots are generally made of terracotta, glazed pottery or plastic, and resemble an urn with lipped planting holes around the sides. There is nothing to choose between terracotta and plastic as far as growing herbs successfully is concerned, but terracotta, even that which is sold as frost-resistant, often cracks and flakes in frosty weather, particularly when it has been outdoors for a year or two. Plastic ones require less watering, but need more care to avoid the herbs lower down becoming waterlogged.

Herb pots come in several sizes, but the smallest ones, which are little more than big jars, can only hold such small amounts of compost that they are really only suitable for regular plantings of single annual species, like parsley, basil or dill, even though they may actually be described as 'herb pots' when they are sold. They may also be sold as 'crocus pots', which is possibly a better description.

A successful herb pot should not require total replanting every year, although it may need some refurbishment from time to time. It should last up to about five years before it needs cleaning out completely and starting again from scratch. To avoid the necessity for frequent replanting, you need a herb pot no smaller than 30cm (1ft) tall by 30cm (1ft) in diameter at its widest point. A pot like this is often confusingly called a 'strawberry pot', though in fact it is far too small to raise strawberries, which need plenty of root space to produce a good crop of fruit.

The standard herb pot will usually have about eight holes around the sides, staggered so that no two holes come directly on top of each other so that the ones nearer the top do not smother those underneath, with a top opening around 20cm (8in) wide internally to allow for easy filling and planting. This will enable you to grow at least nine different herbs (eight round the sides plus one in the top), although depending on variety you may be able to get more than one in the top.

You can use either culinary or aromatic herbs in your pot. It is possible to mix culinary and aromatic herbs together, but it is probably better if you have one pot for herbs you use in the kitchen, and another for the ones you are not likely to eat.

PLANTING UP

Most herbs like Mediterranean growing conditions – that is, an open, free-draining soil and a position in full sun. The nearest suitable thing in a proprietary compost that you are likely to find easily is alpine compost, which is a soil-based medium with extra grit added to it. Herbs will grow well in this, but a good substitute is John Innes No 2 with a little extra sharp sand and grit.

Place some drainage material like broken crocks or crumbled polystyrene packing blocks in the base of the pot before adding any compost, but do not make this too deep or you will not be able to get enough compost in to take the root balls of the plants in the lowest holes.

Correct watering is probably the most tricky part of keeping your herb pot happy, as you may find that, in keeping the top of the container damp enough, the herbs lower down get over-wet. You can remedy this to some extent by placing a piece of plastic sink waste pipe that has had holes drilled in it along its length down the centre of the pot before you start to fill it with compost. Water is poured down this when the pot becomes dry and all parts of the container will then receive the same amount at the same time. The pipe itself should be kept free of compost or the device will not work.

Add compost to just below the lowest hole, then plant your first herbs. Choose young specimens so the roots will go through the holes easily. The planted herb will be at an angle of about 45°, with the root buried in the layer of compost you have just put in. As the herbs grow, they will straighten themselves.

Top up with more compost until you reach the next hole and repeat the process with more herbs until you reach the top. Some compost will escape through the planted holes as you work upwards, but this is nothing to worry about as it will stop when the roots of the herbs start to bind the compost.

CHOOSING THE RIGHT PLANTS

If you want to keep your pot growing from year to year, you need to choose your herbs carefully. Invasive kinds, such as tarragon and particularly mint, are definitely 'out' as they will start popping up everywhere in the pot. Also unsuitable are herbs that will grow too tall no matter how much trimming back they get, such as fennel and lovage. However, if you grow these individually in attractive pots, you can create an effective display by grouping them with a herb pot or pots and/or a herb wheel to give a truly container-grown herb garden.

Your pot should not only supply you with a good selection of herbs, but look decorative as well. For the best visual effect, variegated and ornamental-leaved forms should be used, although if you have a good selection of varieties with attractive foliage, some common varieties can also be included. The flavour of ornamental-leaved forms is usually the same, though sometimes not quite as strong.

Herbs for the lower layers should be ones liking the most moisture and must not grow so tall and bushy that they choke the ones further up. The middle holes can contain bushy herbs that you can keep under control by regular clipping, while the holes nearest the top are best suited to compact species and miniature varieties.

The mouth of the pot may be treated in two different ways. Either two or three kinds of herbs with compatible habits can be combined together, or a well-trained, single plant of a shrubby herb, clipped into a formal or semi-formal shape, may be used. The top may also be used for growing annual or biennial herbs that need replacing on a regular basis.

SUITABLE PLANTS FOR HERB POTS AND WHEELS
(see Appendix 2 for descriptions and uses)

Culinary herbs for the base of the pot
Variegated forms of lemon balm, salad burnet, English mace.

Culinary herbs for middle holes
Sages, oreganos, *Thymus* 'Porlock'.

Culinary herbs for top holes
Dwarf thymes (eg *Thymus serpyllum*, *T. x citriodorus*, *T. doefleri*); golden feverfew.

Culinary herbs for the mouth of pot (also suitable for small 'crocus-pot'-type containers)
Chives, parsley, basil, dill, coriander, cumin.

Shrubby herbs for planting as single specimens in the pot mouth
Rosemary, bay, lemon verbena, hyssop.

Aromatic herbs for the base of pot
Chamomile, monarda, Corsican mint.

Aromatic herbs suitable for sides of pot
Feverfew, *Artemesia schmidtiana* 'nana', pennyroyal.

Aromatic herbs as specimens for the top opening of pot
Shrubby artemesias, lavenders, curry plant, cotton lavender.

TIP
If you want to include invasive herbs, such as mints, in a herb pot, mixed herb tub, hanging basket or window box, plant a young specimen in a small plastic pot, with the bottom cut out and the rim slightly proud of the compost. Cut back all runners as they appear and they will remain under control for a couple of seasons.

CARING FOR A HERB POT

The container should be stood on pot feet or pieces of tile to raise it off the paving. This will prevent the drainage hole or holes becoming blocked. Keep the compost damp but not too moist – very wet conditions will shorten the life of the herbs considerably. If you have used a good, soil-based compost, very little feeding will be needed the first season. During subsequent summers, a liquid feed should be given.

To keep the plants looking good, they will need to be clipped and cut back regularly during the growing season to produce low, bushy, well-shaped specimens with plenty of healthy, young foliage. If the plants are allowed to become out-grown or woody, the overall effect of the pot will be lost.

For herbs to produce the essential oils that give them their individual, characteristic flavours and scents, they should receive plenty of warm, summer sunshine. This will also ripen the stems so they cope better with winter conditions. Always give your herb pot the most open, sunny position you can find and turn it regularly to ensure that all sides are receiving an equal amount of light.

THE HERB WHEEL

This is another method of growing a lot of herbs in a minimum amount of space. The 'wheel' can be made of treated timber or bricks, the idea being that one or two different herbs are planted in the spaces between the spokes of the wheel to give a formal, ornamental layout. Very elaborate spiral structures can be built, which are capable of containing an enormous number of herbs for the ground space they occupy, but you will probably be able to get as many herbs as you want into a simple wheel-shape.

Herb containers made of terracotta and plastic and based on this idea are now widely available. These are circular or semi-circular and are divided into small compartments that will take just one herb plant each. They make an effective substitute for, or attractive complement to, a conventional herb pot and are possibly easier to maintain, although complications can arise if you are watering automatically as each compartment will require a dripper of its own. The advantage of the herb wheel is that,

as it is divided into individual segments, it is possible to use mints and other invasive herbs in the planting since they can be contained within their own segment.

Herb Hanging Baskets

I am not ashamed to admit it – I love hanging baskets. I have dozens of them at home, all watered and fed automatically so they make as little extra work as possible. They give us great pleasure, and are much admired.

I make no attempt to co-ordinate colours, textures or varieties. No doubt many would consider them vulgar, but they work well on the white walls of our cottage and the surrounding timberwork, so if they are in 'bad taste', it really does not worry me.

However, I am the first to admit that those who prefer a more subdued approach have a point. Pastel colours and foliage in gentle shades of grey and blue have a calming effect on the sensitivities and there are many instances where cool, tranquil plantings are much more acceptable than my vibrant approach.

The obvious way to achieve this is with container and bedding plants in pale and pastel shades, but an even more inspiring method is to use herbs. There are so many with foliage (and, in

some instances, flowers) in serene shades that superb results can be achieved with no more effort and cost than by using blowsy bedding subjects, to say nothing of the fact that there are bound to be some species in the planting that can be used in the kitchen or as ingredients in pot pourri.

CHOOSING THE BASKET

The most striking effect is obtained by using an open-sided, wire basket, although if you are prepared to spend the money, there are a very few excellent, imitation terracotta, solid-sided hanging containers available.

Large, well-finished, solid baskets can be quite successful if planted with five or six really pretty herbs – for instance, tricolore sage, curry plant, variegated pineapple mint, variegated lemon balm and pot marjoram, with nasturtiums and *Thymus serpyllum* round the outside to soften the edge.

However, for a really stunning basket, there is nothing to beat a wire one where the sides, as well as the top, have been planted so closely that none of the container can be seen at all once the plants have grown up a little. Use the largest basket you can find – certainly no smaller than 35cm (14in) in diameter. The deeper the basket, the more layers of plants you can get round the sides. You will make life easier for yourself if you use a basket with a very open wire framework. Although in theory this makes the basket weaker, in practice I have never had any problems with such a design of basket breaking and small holes do make it extremely difficult to plant up the sides with anything bigger than the smallest rooted cuttings.

BEST HANGING BASKET HERBS

Always start off with small specimens. These will be easier to work through the sides and, although the basket may look a little sparse when newly planted, young plants will grow away more quickly and will soon produce the desired effect.

In choosing suitable varieties, the same principles apply as when planting a conventional, ornamental basket – that is, plants with a more lax habit should be used around the sides and top edges; bushy and upright ones are more suitable for the top. If you can arrange to plant something trailing, like nasturtiums, pennyroyal or purslane at or near the base of the chains, they can be trained upwards as they grow to make the basket look even more spectacular.

Unlike most container herb plantings, I do not recommend that you attempt to keep your herb basket from year to year, although it is possible if you use one with solid sides and use only hardy, perennial varieties. Your main aim is for an early, good visual effect over a comparatively short period during the warmer months of the year. This means that you will have to plant much closer than is good for the herbs if they are to achieve a long, happy and healthy life.

In order to include as wide a range of foliage texture as possible, you should include annual herbs with interesting leaves, like dill and coriander. Even if you were to save your basket for another year, these would need replanting as they die at the end of summer. It is therefore best to have a clean start at the beginning of the season, when all plants will be equally healthy and at the same stage of development.

Your selection should be as diverse in foliage colour and texture as possible, so you will usually have to mix culinary, aromatic and medicinal herbs, but without spoiling the overall effect you should be able to include ornamental varieties of several of the flavours you tend to use most in cooking.

As a guide to estimating the number of herbs you will need, to achieve a balance between getting good results in as short a time as possible and the kind of serious overcrowding which will considerably shorten the life of your basket, young plants should be spaced about 5cm (2in) apart, both round the sides and at the top.

SOME SUITABLE HERBS FOR THE SIDES AND TOP EDGE OF A HANGING BASKET

SIDES AND TOP EDGE

Curly mint, apple mint, ginger mint, variegated pineapple mint. (But see tip on planting invasive subjects on page 73.)
Basil (all varieties), creeping savory, oregano, purslane, tarragon, *Thymus serpyllum*, *Thymus x citriodorus*, nasturtium, Corsican mint (*Mentha requinii*), pennyroyal, chamomile.

BASKET TOP

Coriander (young seedlings), dill (young seedlings), hyssop, lavender (dwarf forms), sage (all forms), feverfew, parsley (young seedlings), salad burnet, bushy varieties of thyme, pot marigold (dwarf varieties), wild pansy (heartease), artemesia ('Powis Castle', young plants), curry plant, *Santolina incana* 'Nana'; *Santolina virens*.

PLANTING UP A WIRE BASKET WITH HERBS

Place a good layer of moss in the base of the basket, and at the same time, line the sides until you reach the point at which you want to plant your first herbs – usually about 5–7.5cm (2–3in) above the bottom. Use enough moss to make the lining thick enough to prevent compost from washing out in the early stages, before the roots have started to bind it. Use a good, general purpose, soil-less compost and add to just below the present level of the moss. Firm gently but do not compact.

Work the first layer of plants through the lined basket sides. If there is enough room between the wires, it is best to push the roots through from the outside. Where the side wires are close together, you may find it easier to plant from the inside out, in which case you should wrap the tops of the herbs in thin cardboard to make it easier to push the tops through the sides and prevent the young shoots being damaged.

Line a further 5–7.5cm (2–3in) of the basket side with moss, add compost and plant a second ring of herbs as before. Make sure that these are not directly above those in the first layer or they may hang down and smother them. Finish lining the basket sides with moss and add more compost until the basket is full to about 4–5cm (1–2in) of the rim.

Plant up the top. Firm the compost and add more if necessary until the level is just below that of the top rim of the basket. Water thoroughly and place it on a level surface at ground level outdoors for about a week to allow it to settle down. It may then be hung in its summer position. It should always be given a light, sunny sheltered position.

AFTERCARE

Herb hanging baskets are treated in exactly the same way as others – that is, they should be fed regularly and never be allowed to dry out. They will require less water at the beginning and end of the season than during high summer. Any liquid or soluble, general purpose or specific container fertiliser is suitable.

All hanging baskets, no matter what they contain, will require a little 'servicing' from time to time. In the case of bedding baskets, this will comprise regular dead-heading to keep the plants in peak condition. With herb baskets, routine care mainly consists of trimming back any herbs that are beginning to outgrow the others, so that a balanced appearance is maintained. If the baskets contain flowering plants, such as nasturtiums or pot marigolds, these will have to be dead-headed from time to time, otherwise, being hardy annuals, they will set seed and stop flowering. However, if you like the flavour of pickled nasturtium seeds, you can allow some seed to form. This is harvested before they harden and dry off, and so the plants can recover and continue to make flower buds.

A Permanent Herb Window Box

There comes a time when, even if you are the most enthusiastic patio gardener, you decide it is time to cut down on routine jobs. One good way to do this is to convert the window boxes you religiously replant twice yearly with spring and summer bedding into permanently stocked features. Perennial herbs are ideal subjects for this since, if you choose the right varieties, they can look as good in winter as they do in summer with much less effort.

FIRST, GET YOUR WINDOW BOX

Window boxes lend a whole new dimension to patio gardening. If you fancy the idea but have never tried window box gardening before and therefore have nothing to convert, here are a few tips. Always have the biggest box you can accommodate – the plants will thrive in it so much better.

If you want to grow herbs, make sure the box receives plenty of sun.

It is better to fix the box under the windowsill, rather than on it. This will enable you to open the window if you need to and it is much easier to fix a box firmly to the wall than it is to the sill. If you leave a gap between the top of the box and the bottom of the sill, you will be able to let your plants grow taller before you start to obstruct the light entering the room.

You can either use purpose-made wooden boxes or adapt plastic troughs with special window box holders. Wooden boxes keep the roots warmer in winter and can be made to individual requirements, but must be treated with a plant-friendly wood preservative before use. Even so, the bottoms will eventually start to rot. Wooden boxes can either be fixed direct to the wall or screwed to brackets that are fixed to the wall.

Plastic boxes come in a limited range of sizes and designs and do not usually hold as much compost. Good quality ones made from UV-stabilised plastic will last a decade or more without maintenance, although the colour or finish may deteriorate over the years. It is vital that whatever type of box you use, it is very firmly fixed to the wall before you start to plant up. Once up and running, it will be extremely heavy

CHOOSING THE BEST PERENNIAL HERBS FOR A WINDOW BOX

Use young plants, but they should not be too small or you will be tempted to overcrowd in order to achieve an instant effect. For a window box intended to last more than a single season, individual specimens need some room for growth. When selecting varieties, look for effective foliage combinations above all else. As with hanging baskets, trailing and lax plants can be used at the front and sides to hang down and partially cover the faces of the box.

Try to pick herbs that retain at least some foliage in winter. If there is something you particularly want that is not evergreen, position it against something that is. This will take the eye off the bare stems when the plant has lost its leaves.

You can combine culinary, aromatic and medicinal herbs, but be careful not to include annual and biennial ones as your box will not establish evenly if you have to replant several parts of it regularly.

Do not use invasive herbs, such as mint, as these will spread throughout the whole box before the end of the first summer and will be impossible to sort out without removing everything and starting again.

Try to position your box near an opening window so you can enjoy the scent of the herbs in warm sunshine, but remember that, if the window does open, you must not include anything in your box that will get too tall. In fact, taller herbs should be avoided in all cases since, if they grow up and obscure the glass, you will lose a lot of light. No window box plants look good when viewed from the inside outwards.

Herb window box in winter and summer

GOOD HERBS FOR PERMANENTLY PLANTED WINDOW BOXES

Creeping savory, oregano, variegated forms of lemon balm, thymes, Corsican mint (*Mentha requinii*), pennyroyal, chamomile, hyssop, lavender, sage (all forms), feverfew, salad burnet, curry plant, *Santolina incana* 'Nana', *Artemesia schmidtiana* 'Nana'

PLANTING THE BOX

Lemon balm

Make sure the box has plenty of holes before you begin. Plastic plant troughs often do not have holes but have indentations in the plastic where the holes should be if they are needed. Make sure that these are drilled out if necessary.

Place a shallow layer of broken crocks, coarse gravel or other drainage material in the bottom, then fill the box to within 5–7.5cm (2–3in) of the top. Use a John Innes-type compost, made more free-draining with the addition of a little sharp sand or fine grit. Better still, use a proprietary alpine compost.

Position the herbs on the surface of the compost and check for effect. The distance apart will depend on the types you are using, but the plants should not be closer to each other than 12–15cm (5-6in). If you want your boxes to last for several years without replanting, you are better to use fewer specimens and allow them to develop properly. Five or six bushy, healthy subjects may look far more attractive than a dozen overcrowded ones, all fighting for survival, in the same sized box.

Plant the herbs so the tops of the root balls are about 4cm (1.5in) below the top of the box. Add compost so the surface of the root ball is just below the surface of the compost after the planting has been firmed in gently.

Water thoroughly until it runs through the drainage holes. You will not need to water again for some time, particularly if you have planted the box in early or late in the year.

AFTERCARE

Watering is the main priority. In the early stages, you must be careful not to over-water since a soil-based compost dries out less quickly than a peat-based one and young specimens will use moisture less rapidly. Herbs suitable for window boxes will not tolerate over-watering even for short periods. Rather than lay down hard-and-fast times when to water, it is better to check how dry the compost is by inserting a finger carefully into the top layer to see if it is still damp.

You will not need to feed during the first season, as your compost should contain enough fertiliser to see the box through its first summer. After that, a general-purpose liquid feed should be applied regularly from early April to September.

The herbs will need pruning or cutting back on an individual basis when they need it, usually if they are getting too tall or if they are threatening to smother their neighbours. The plants in a mature window box will tend to merge into each other, so you will get an overall effect of a mass of foliage colour and texture.

Herb Edgings

It is quite common to see lavender used as edgings for paths, knot gardens, ornamental beds, borders and the like, but it is often not realised that many herbs can be used to edge parts of the garden, to give widely differing effects.

You will get different results depending on the type of herbs you choose. For example, evergreen shrubby herbs (and one or two herbaceous ones) can be planted in a formal strip to define the edge of the patio or flank a path. Shorter, woody kinds may also be used to edge borders and beds, but this can also be done with herbaceous perennial herbs, which have the advantage of needing to be cut down at least once a year when the border is given its annual tidy-up.

The same area can, however, be edged with annual and biennial herbs to give a completely different feel. Since all herbs are easily raised from either seed, cuttings or root division, you can, if you wish, try one idea for a year or two, then change the edging for something quite different – you will be amazed at how easy it is to alter the look of an area in this way.

Another way to use rows of herbs on the patio is as a summer screen. If you want something quick-growing to hide you from your neighbour during the summer, but are not too bothered about the rest of the year, some of the taller, architectural herbs are just the job.

With a few exceptions, herbs suitable for use as edgings and dwarf hedging should be given a sunny, sheltered warm spot and free-draining soil. If your ground is on the heavy side, open it up first by digging in horticultural sharp sand until the texture looks more open (do not use builders' sharp sand, which is often much too alkaline to grow plants in successfully). Most herbs, with one or two exceptions mentioned later on in this section, will not do well under other plants or in partial or total shade.

ANNUAL EDGINGS

Basil 'Red Rubin'

This is something else that the gardener who has always edged everything every summer with blue lobelia and white alyssum might like to try. Annual and biennial herbs can be raised in the spring by sowing the seed in trays of seed compost, then pricking out the seedlings into modules, small plant pots or fibre pots when large enough to handle. When the plants have grown enough to make an impact, they are planted out along the bed or border edge, about 7.5–8cm (6–8in) apart. If a greenhouse or something similar is not available, it is possible to raise the plants on the patio in a cold frame or under cloches or bell jars providing you wait until the weather has warmed up (around mid-April). Perhaps the two best temporary herbs for this purpose are parsley and basil. Varieties of parsley with finely cut or curled leaves, like 'Afro' or 'Curlina', give the most visual impact and the taste is little different from the plain-leaved forms that are usually recommended for cooking purposes. Parsley will tolerate partial, though not total, shade.

For the best effect, green basil should be planted in blocks and alternated with a purple variety like 'Red Rubin'.

Sweet marjoram may also be used in the same way, although it does give a rather green, leafy effect. It is not a good idea to mix entirely different herbs (for instance, basil, parsley and marjoram) in a single edging run, as the definition is lost.

You will need to trim these herbs back once or twice during the summer or they will start to look untidy. Young foliage always has the best flavour, so trim back before the leaves start to look old and tired. You will get huge amounts of herbs from quite a short row each time you cut them back. The best way to store them is to rinse and dry them, then freeze the lot – leaves and stems – in polythene bags and break off what you want for cooking just when you need it. Providing you do it immediately, you can crumble the herbs, which will be very brittle while frozen, straight into the dish you are preparing, doing away with the tedious job of chopping them up. You will not be able to use them for garnish, as herbs lose structure once frozen.

In the autumn, you can remove your summer herbs and clean the ground up where they grew. If, like me, you can't bear to live with even a temporary empty space in the garden, you can replace them with spring bedding plants such as winter pansies, forget-me-nots or polyanthus, which should be just about past their best when you need to replant your parsley or whatever the following year.

PERENNIAL HERBS FOR LOW EDGINGS

The best perennial herbs are those with a compact and, preferably, evergreen habit. They may die down at the end of summer, but should leave at least a rosette of leaves to provide some interest during winter. They should not be invasive (like mint, for instance), or you can give yourself big problems with other plants nearby.

Most suitable species can be used in the kitchen, but possibly the best, golden feverfew, is really only ornamental. Feverfew self-seeds readily so, starting off with one plant, you should be able to find enough seedlings around the garden within twelve months to make a formal edging. If you do not want the plants to seed once they have been replanted, you must cut the flower heads off before they start to fade. It is a good idea, however, to leave a few plants to seed, as feverfew is not usually a long-lived herb.

Pot marjoram, especially the golden and variegated forms, makes an ideal edging plant. Oregano is really a sub-shrub, but in habit is more like a herbaceous perennial and clipping back regularly will provide an abundance of soft, attractive foliage.

Surplus oregano trimmings can be frozen for future use in the same way as parsley. It also keeps its flavour well if dried quickly in a cooling oven and then stored in airtight tins or jars in a cool, dark cupboard.

Salad burnet is often grown as a salad leaf vegetable, but also makes a good herb edging. In all but the coldest winters, the decorative, basal leaves remain evergreen, while the reddish, ball-shaped flowers are an attractive summer addition. Unlike most herbs, salad burnet will tolerate some shade, so is useful for edging beneath, for example, roses or dwarf shrubs.

The grassy leaves of chives make a first-class summer edging, with pretty, lavender-coloured flower heads as a bonus. Unfortunately, the foliage is not evergreen, so there will be a period from late autumn to early spring when the ground they occupy appears bare. If this does not worry you, however, chives make one of the most useful edgings you can find.

The old-fashioned, cottage garden herb *nepeta* (catmint) can also be used for this purpose. Apart from its aromatic fragrance, its main use appears to be to keep your cat, to say nothing of all the neighbourhood moggies, in a state of ecstasy, but the grey-green leaves and blue-mauve flower spikes are very pretty, even though they tend to flop, so that they require plenty of space.

While on the subject of cottage gardens, the once-popular, highly fragrant medicinal herb chamomile can be planted to form an edging. The common form, *Anthemis nobilis*, produces attractive white flowers, but if you want something low and well-behaved, you should look for the non-flowering form 'Treneague', which is the variety recommended for so-called 'camomile lawns'.

TALLER HERBS FOR FORMAL EDGINGS AND LOW HEDGES

To be really successful, herbs for this purpose should be neat, compact, and capable of being clipped or shaped with shears or a hedge trimmer once or twice during summer. The ever-popular lavender is still one of the best aromatic shrubs for low hedges and formal edgings. All varieties may be used – if you are looking for height, choose a taller cultivar like the purple-flowered 'Willow Vale', pink 'Miss Katherine' or the old-fashioned English lavender. Where space is at a premium, plant a dwarf or compact-growing form like 'Little Lottie', 'Munstead' or 'Little Lady'.

Lavender must be trimmed at least once a year during the warmer weather, otherwise its life is shortened considerably.

NOTE

Comfrey (Symphytum) is a medicinal herb which can be toxic if absorbed or ingested, but can be composted to make a nutritional soil conditioner, or steeped in water and used as a liquid fertiliser. Some low growing varieties particularly Symphytum grand florum, and its several cultivations, can be used as a 'bomb-proof' shade tolerant edging.

Never cut back into hard wood, or the bushes will not grow again.

Hyssop can be treated in the same way as lavender and if clipped regularly gives a very similar effect. For something absolutely different in appearance, but requiring the same method of cultivation and aftercare, try winter savory.

For a change, you could use *santolina* (cotton lavender). The best forms for clipping are the grey-leaved *S. incana* and its more dwarf form, *S. incana* 'Nana' and the bright green, profuse flowering *Santolina virens*. If you want a less formal habit, you should plant the larger-leaved, more open *Santolina neapolitana*, or you can achieve a similar effect with *Helichrysum angustifolium* (curry plant), which gives off a very mouth-watering aroma if you are hungry, although if you are out-of-sorts it can turn your stomach!

Rosemary can also be clipped to form low hedges and edges. The best cultivar for formal work is possibly the upright 'Miss Jessup's Variety'. This will bush out with regular trimming but never loses its compact habit.

Sage is not often used in this way, yet makes a good, low, shrubby edging. All forms can be used. Regular cutting back gives the plants a much longer life than if they were left to their own devices. Bushy thymes, like 'Porlock', and the widely available common thyme, can be planted and treated in much the same way for a lower but still shrubby edging.

The shrubby artemesias make very good low hedges if a gentler effect is required. Clipping will keep them low and within bounds, but will not tame their soft, flowing foliage. The variety that I find works best is the non-flowering form 'Powis Castle', but *Artemesia arborescens* and its several cultivars are also successful.

Two taller, aromatic shrubs are also worth looking at if more height is needed. One is the narrowly upright *perowskia* (Russian sage), and the other is *phlomis* (Jerusalem sage). Russian sage is useful where ground space is limited, while Jerusalem sage can make quite a large hedge if left unchecked, but can be kept within bounds to better effect by pruning back a couple of times a season with secateurs to encourage plenty of young growth from low down the bushes.

Lemon verbena and sweet bay can also be used for a slightly taller edging as they will clip to almost any height and width if this is done regularly from the outset.

Agastache anise hyssop and Korean mint, although herbaceous perennials that die down in winter, are also candidates for this type of planting. The plants regularly provide a good many stocky stems with lots of interesting, toothed foliage and the abundant flowers produced over a long period are useful for attracting beneficial insects and bringing the drowsy hum of bees on a warm summer's day to the sunny patio. *Agastache* is easily raised from seed in spring in the same way as a half-hardy annual, and will flower the first summer.

HERBS FOR SCREENS

Agastache rugosa

There are some excellent, tall herbs that, planted in the right places, will give you all the summer privacy you need. For patio cultivation, it is best to grow them in a designated bed, created by leaving out a strategically placed area of paving.

The best herbs for the job are ones with sturdy stems requiring little or no staking. The stems should also be well clothed to block a view successfully. Most of these are larger members of the parsley family, like angelica, fennel and lovage, but you could also consider the attractive-flowered costmary. The drawback of this herb is that it has a creeping rootstock that can become invasive if allowed to grow unchecked. However, if you contain its roots in some way, for example by growing the screen in a large trough, it has advantages over fennel and its near relations in that it does not die down in winter, so affords some year-round privacy and, furthermore, the leaves can be used as a mint substitute in winter cooking.

Herbs as Specimens

Many shrubby herbs are amongst the most architectural of plants and make ideal single specimens for attractive tubs, pots and similar containers. They are excellent for the smaller garden and patio grower since most can be clipped or trained to shape and size. Another argument in favour of growing them in this way is that some herbs of dubious hardiness, such as rosemary, sweet bay and curry plant, actually become hardier if they are regularly pruned, providing it is always the young foliage which is clipped back.

Certain herbaceous herbs can also be given the single pot specimen treatment if they cannot be included in mixed plantings. Amongst these are those of anti-social habit, such as mint, costmary and tarragon, and also ones that, although they are attractive of habit or leaf or both, will grow too large. Examples of these are agastache, angelica, fennel (particularly the bronze-leaved form), lovage, balm and sweet Cicely.

Remember that most herbaceous perennial herbs will die down in winter, so pots of these need grouping with evergreen, shrubby kinds that will attract the eye away from the seemingly empty containers.

A LONG LIFE AND A HAPPY ONE

Nearly all herbs suitable for pot cultivation are long-lived. Routine work can therefore be reduced to a minimum if they are potted up correctly at the outset.

Use the right container: although most plants, herbs included, will grow happily for a short time in a plastic pot, they are more likely to last for many years without disturbance if a ceramic, stone, ornamental concrete or wooden pot or tub is used. This will protect the roots to a large extent from wide fluctuations in temperature and, if manufactured from good quality material, is likely to last longer than plastic, which biodegrades in sunlight after a while (although the best quality, heavy duty plastic can be a good substitute, and is much easier to handle). Terracotta can flake or crack in extremely cold conditions, and allows the roots to dry out more rapidly, so is not the best choice.

Choose the right compost: it is tempting to use soil-less, multi-purpose compost for this kind of job. While herbs will grow well in it for the first year or so, it becomes played out very quickly and you will find that most plants will start to deteriorate after this time, no matter how much care and attention you give them. Furthermore, the texture of soil-less compost is not the kind of medium in which most herbs would thrive in their natural environment. Far better is to use a good, proprietary, John Innes-

Baytree with
edible flowers
and beans

type compost, and I find this can be improved even further for herbs if you add around one quarter by volume of sharp sand. This creates a very open medium which the roots will take to readily, although it is very free-draining and so the pots must be watched carefully for drying out.

Pick the right spot: these plants need warmth and sun for the maximum production of aromatic oils, so the pots should be positioned in a sunny, sheltered place. Many herbs that are good candidates for pot culture are grey-leaved and will only survive for more than a season if they are given full light. Plants such as lavender, *santolina*, *artemesia* and curry plant will rapidly become spindly in shade, and will usually die during the first winter if they do not receive enough sun to ripen the wood properly.

Give good drainage: shrubby herbs, particularly, cannot cope with waterlogged conditions – their roots soon rot in soggy soil or compost. When planting up, provide a layer of coarse drainage material, such as broken crocks, coarse gravel or crumbled polystyrene blocks, in the base of the container before starting to add compost. Raising the container above the paving slightly on pot feet or something similar will reduce the risk of the drainage holes becoming blocked.

Choose the right-sized container: mature plants can be grown in quite large containers, but if you are starting with really small plants, it is better to use smaller pots at the beginning and pot on into larger ones until your specimens are big enough to cope with large containers and the amount of compost they hold. A small specimen in a large pot looks silly and the young root ball often stagnates and starts to rot if faced with more compost than it needs to become established. Unlike most of the herbs we are looking at here, invasive ones, like mint, benefit from regular splitting and repotting as they soon fill any container, whatever the size.

Water sensibly: newly planted specimens will not need watering as often as ones that have been in the same container and compost for several years. It is better to let the compost almost dry out before watering, rather than giving water on a regular basis, which may cause the roots to become too moist.

Feed in moderation: soil-based compost contains enough fertiliser to see newly planted herbs through several months, after which time they will benefit from a weak liquid feed weekly during the growing season (April to late September). Permanently planted specimens can be top-dressed each spring with a slow-release, dry fertiliser (such as Vitax Q4). This should be forked into the top layer if possible. It can be advantageous to older specimen plants that have been in the same container and compost for several years if the top few inches of compost is removed annually in March and replaced with new John Innes No 3.

GETTING THE BEST EFFECT

Pot-grown herbs can be best displayed in one of two ways. Larger specimens in big pots need to make an individual statement and can therefore be positioned singly to good effect or in pairs to accent a sunny doorway or access to the patio or something similar. Single herbs in smaller pots need grouping for the best results. A good feature can be created by grouping together several pots of different sizes, styles and colours (the more, the better) containing herbs with as wide a range of foliage effects and colours as possible. You can add a finishing touch by topping the pots with ornamental chipping and gravel. This is as functional as it is ornamental in that it helps to conserve moisture at the top of the containers, which is where the pots tend to dry out most. Groups of herbs in medium and small pots look good placed in groups around the edge of a formal or semi-formal pool, where you get the benefit of reflections in the water.

HERBS SUITABLE FOR CLIPPING OR PRUNING AS LARGE SPECIMENS

Sweet bay, rosemary, artemesia (shrubby types), lemon verbena, Jerusalem sage.

SMALLER, SHRUBBY HERBS SUITABLE FOR GROWING IN SINGLE SPECIMENS IN MEDIUM AND SMALL CONTAINERS

Lavender, cotton lavender, curry plant, sage; hyssop, winter savory.

The Two Metres by One Metre Herb Garden

If you are considering laying or revamping a sunny patio, you might like to think about leaving out sufficient slabs to give you a bed two metres long by one metre wide (or two yards by one yard, if you prefer it). This will, in fact, give you quite enough area to grow most of the herbs you are likely to need, in an informal layout that will be just as attractive as a border of bedding plants or the currently fashionable 'Mediterranean-style' bed. Of course, you can plant the bed up in a formal design, using larger numbers of fewer herbs – taste usually dictates which method to choose.

These dimensions work equally well with a raised bed, if this would be more suited to the style of your patio. In this case, there is no need to leave out the paving, and the raised bed could be built straight off the slabs, but if so, it is important that regularly spaced gaps are left in the mortar at ground level so that the bed can drain properly.

This kind of bed is just as easy to maintain as any ornamental planting if the spacings and planting are correct in the first place. Position it in the sunniest place you can find and place the plants close enough to cover the soil (thus eventually eliminating weeding), but far enough apart to prevent the herbs choking each other after a season or two. You need to know the size and spread that the herbs will attain before you start and I find that drawing a plan first helps you to get the planting right first time.

THE TWO METRES BY ONE METRE HERB GARDEN

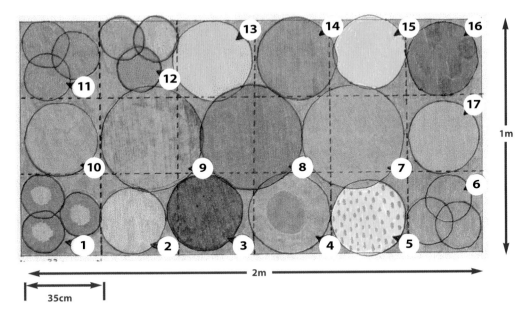

1 chives
2 Golden Oregano
3 Chocolate peppermint
4 Hyssop
5 Variegated pineapple mint
6 Thyme 'Doone Valley'
   (lemon)
7 Lavender 'Sawyers'
8 Rosemary
   'Miss Jessops Var'
9 Purple sage

10 Parsley
11 Thyme 'Porlock'
12 Pot marigold 'Fiesta
   Gitana'
13 Golden lemon balm
14 Apple mint
15 Golden feverfew
16 Green and purple
   leaved basil
17 Dill

BEFORE YOU START

As with herbs grown in other ways, one basic essential is to make
sure the soil is right – open but not impoverished and free-draining but not too light or shallow. If you are starting from scratch,
your own soil in the vicinity of the patio may be adequate. If not,
it will pay you to excavate the area of the bed to a depth of about
38–40cm (15in) and replace the existing earth with good quality
topsoil (adding a little sharp sand if it needs opening up a bit). It
is wise to check the drainage first by tipping a couple of buckets

of water into the excavation and noting how long the water takes to drain away. If it takes more than an hour or so, you will need to improve the subsoil drainage by making holes all over the base with a crowbar and filling them with coarse grit. Once you are satisfied that the water does drain in a reasonable time, you can then refill the area with new soil.

If you want to make this kind of bed in an existing patio, you are likely to find a lot of rubbish when you remove the paving, such as sand, hardcore and poor subsoil. This should be removed and replaced with similar soil to that described above, paying special attention to the drainage as before.

A raised bed of this size may also be filled with good, open topsoil. To ensure the best possible drainage, about 8–10cm (3–4in) of well-broken rubble should be placed in the base of the bed before filling.

SUITABLE SUBJECTS

To look right, the plants need to be of a type that will eventually grow to a medium size. This means that herbs that grow very tall, like lovage and fennel, will not be suitable. Some herbaceous types, like lemon balm, tarragon and mint, if you intend to leave them to their own devices, should be positioned in the middle of a bed intended to be viewed from all sides. If not, once they start to flower, they will hide more modest-growing ones nearer the centre.

However, as you will probably want to pick these more often than some of the others, they need to be in an accessible spot. The best solution is to cut the plants back when they start getting too tall, so you are provided with a regular supply of young, attractive, well-flavoured foliage.

Unlike mixed herbs in small containers, there is no need to exclude those with a normally invasive habit when the planting area is as large as this, as their anti-social antics can be curtailed by planting them in buckets or large, plastic pots with the bottoms removed. Make sure that the rims are left proud so they do not get covered with soil, or the herb runners will soon escape and colonise the surrounding soil.

Where possible, use herbs with attractive leaves – brightly or attractively coloured, variegated or with a pleasant shape or texture. Do not confine your choice to varieties that are grey, cream, gold, purple, blue or some other unusual colour, however, since the strategic use of green is necessary to get the most out of foliage of other shades. When positioning the herbs, pay particular attention to how each blends with its neighbours. For example, two herbs in identical shades of grey would be better separated by one or more green-leaved varieties.

GETTING THE TIMING RIGHT

I like to plant a herb bed in spring or early summer, so the plants can become established before the winter. Herbs planted late in the summer often produce growth that is less hardy and will be damaged by frost. Very young specimens planted late in the season often die during their first winter in a herb bed.

ADDING THE FINISHING TOUCHES

Once the herbs are planted, the soil surface can be covered with pea shingle or ornamental chippings. This looks attractive, prevents most weeds growing until the plants are large enough to act as their own ground cover and keeps enough moisture in the earth to stop the young specimens drying out in hot weather – the temperature at ground level on a sunny, paved area can be extremely high because of the reflected heat from the slabs.

AFTERCARE

Shrubby herbs, like sage, lavender and rosemary, need regular light pruning to keep them young and a good shape. The best times to do this are in mid-spring (usually April) when new shoots are starting to grow and in late July, so they can make more

French lavender

leaves before the frosts. They will not always need pruning twice a year, only when they start to look untidy and lose their shape. The easiest way to prune is to clip the bush all over with shears, taking care not to cut too far back, and particularly not into woody stems. If you prefer it, you can use secateurs, removing each unwanted shoot in turn. This takes longer, but the effect is better as you do not clip through individual leaves and so you get less of a 'shaved head' effect. The prunings can be dried or frozen, or used as an ingredient of pot pourri.

Herbaceous herbs will need periodic cutting back as already described, to keep them tidy, of a manageable size and encourage the production of the best-flavoured shoots. Invasive kinds, like mint, will require removing from their open-bottomed containers, usually annually in spring, splitting, and replanting.

Annual and biennial sorts should be removed from the bed when they die or start to look untidy and replanted the following year, usually in early summer. Always remove premature flowering shoots unless you are growing a particular herb for its edible flowers, like borage or heartsease. Some temporary herbs, particularly dill and coriander, run to seed almost as soon as they are planted. If this happens, remove the flowering stems and apply a local application of a high-nitrogen fertiliser, such as dried blood, only to the area around the plant causing problems. If you prevent them running to seed, the leaves will be well-flavoured until the plants die off before the end of the summer. Dill and coriander may, of course, be allowed to set seed later in the season. This is harvested when it starts to turn brown but before it falls from the plant. It is then thoroughly dried and can be stored in a screw-topped jar in a cool, dark cupboard and used in cooking over winter as required.

FEEDING

Shrubby herbs should not be overfed, particularly with a high-nitrogen fertiliser, because they may then become susceptible to frost. Annual, biennial and perennial herbaceous types require more feeding, so a good compromise is to feed annually in spring with a light dressing of a dry, slow-release, balanced fertiliser. This will dispense plant food little and often throughout the summer when it is needed, without encouraging too much lush top growth.

THE LONG-TERM VIEW

Generally speaking, herbs that are shrubs or sub-shrubs do not have a very long life, so it is a good idea after a few years to take cuttings and replace the parent plants when they begin to look too woody, untidy or unhealthy. To ensure that you produce the best new plants, you should take cuttings – preferably in early summer – before the old herbs begin to look past their best, grow them on for one or two years in pots and then replant. I usually recommend removing a small amount of soil from the hole they occupied and replacing it with new topsoil before replanting.

Window Sill Herbs

If you have read gardening magazines regularly for as long as I have, you will know that, in the 'Jobs for the Week' column some-time during the autumn, there is always a recommendation to 'pot up a few herbs to bring indoors to see you through the winter'.

Unfortunately, it is not quite as simple as that. For a start, many kitchen herbs that you may use frequently do not, in fact, require bringing indoors at all, since they are hardy evergreen shrubs and quite capable of surviving outside throughout the colder months. Typical examples of these are bay, thyme, rose-mary and sage, which in all but the coldest areas can remain in the same situation that they have occupied all summer provid-ing they have been given optimum growing conditions (plenty of warm sunshine and good, well-drained compost). However, if you live in a very inclement spot, it is a good idea to cover the plants with horticultural fleece or old net curtains if tempera-tures are likely to fall very low. A good alternative is to keep

small plants of herbs such as these in a cold frame, but this must be well-ventilated or the leaves will rot. In fact, unless it is extremely frosty, you can leave the cold frame lid open or off altogether, particularly during the daytime. Evergreen, shrubby herbs will see the winter through much better given this treatment than if they are too warm and under conditions of reduced light on the kitchen windowsill.

One alternative is to keep them over winter in a cool or unheated conservatory or greenhouse, but they must receive the best light possible. Green algae on the outside of the glass and even heavy condensation on the windows can reduce light levels to a point where most plants will not thrive. Always make sure there is plenty of ventilation.

HERBS FOR POTTING UP

There are relatively few herbs that you can actually dig up from the garden, pot up and grow on in the home over winter. The most suitable are mint, tarragon, chives and lemon balm (although you are not likely to use balm very often during the winter).

These are all plants with a wide-spreading rootstock or, in the case of chives, easily divided, and re-establish themselves quickly when disturbed. Although the recommendation is to pot up in autumn, I prefer to do this no later than August, so they can settle down before being subjected to the unnatural conditions of the family kitchen.

HOW TO POT UP HERBS FROM THE GARDEN

THE POTS

Use pots of a size that will fit comfortably on the windowsill. As you will be looking at them closely for several months, you might like to use ones that are pleasing to the eye, rather than just opt for straightforward, brown plastic ones. There is a wide choice of inexpensive pots available these days, including some very attractive ceramic or terracotta ones – terracotta works well in this kind of situation as the plant roots can breathe better.

THE COMPOST

As these herbs are likely only to be potted up for a limited period, there is no need to use a soil-based compost. A good quality, soil-less compost is quite satisfactory, and will help the divided herbs to establish more quickly.

THE PLANTS

Carefully remove small pieces of the herbs you are potting up with a small trowel. The pieces should be of a size to fit the pots comfortably and allow room for some compost between the roots and the sides of the pots. Trim back the roots slightly with sharp scissors to remove any damaged bits. Cut back all top growth to within a couple of centimetres (an inch) or so of the base.

POTTING UP

Place a small amount of compost in the base of the pot, then introduce the plant. Add compost around the sides, working it into the roots and firming it gently with the fingers. Water well until it runs out of the bottom of the pot. This will settle the compost and make sure there are no air spaces around the roots. Top up with more compost if necessary to leave about 2.5cm (1in) at the top of the pot to make watering easier.

AFTERCARE

If the job was done in late summer, the pots can be left outside for 6–8 weeks in the fresh air. New shoots will appear that should be well enough grown to use indoors from late September onwards. Do not leave the pots outdoors if cold weather is forecast, as the herbs will start to die back naturally like the ones in the open garden.

POSITIONING FOR BEST RESULTS

Herbs always need the best light possible. This is difficult in the average home, but they will grow reasonably well if placed on a south-facing windowsill. If you want a good supply of indoor herbs over winter, their requirements will therefore have to take precedence over their ornamental value. They may look more decorative on a kitchen windowsill facing north looking out onto a high brick wall, but they will do far better in front of the south- or west-facing patio doors in your sitting room. Water carefully and only when necessary. The rate at which the compost will dry out will depend on many factors, but particularly the temperature of the room.

CUTTING THE HERBS

Pick sparingly, a few leaves at a time. It is a good idea to have several pots of the herbs you use most since, once you have removed all the foliage, it will take some time for the plants to grow again. If you intend to use the herbs another year, they should have a resting period after all the shoots have been removed.

WINDOWSILL HERBS FROM SEED

Most of us have bought pots of herbs from the supermarket. They always seem to be bursting with health when you put them in your trolley, but within a short time they have sickened and died, no matter how considerate you have been. It is quite easy to raise the same kinds of herbs yourself from seed. They will usually be much more successful than shop-bought ones since they are acclimatised to your conditions from the outset.

The seed can usually be obtained from any well-known seed company, although you may have to buy some varieties by mail order as it is unlikely that you will find all of them in the garden centre seed racks.

The herbs that lend themselves best to this kind of cultivation are the hardy and half-hardy annuals and biennials which you would normally raise in spring, plant out in early summer and discard at the end of the season. Try chervil, coriander, cumin, dill, basil, parsley, and lemon grass. You will be surprised what a difference freshly grown and picked herbs make to your cooking compared with the dried ones most of us have usually to make do with.

Admittedly, it is easier to start in the spring, when the temperature and level of light are increasing, so for convenience you might like to sow a few pots at this time of year. These can either be grown on indoors, or may be used like half-hardy bedding plants outdoors on the patio. However, all the herbs listed above can be successfully sown later in the season.

For winter use, you should ideally sow during the second half of summer (late July to the end of August). Use 8cm (3 in) plastic plant pots and sow a small pinch of seed in each, using a good quality, soil-less, seed compost. Cover the seed with a very thin layer of compost and dampen the surface carefully, using a hand mister or houseplant watering can fitted with a fine rose.

Place the pots in a cool, light position (in front of the French window or in the conservatory is ideal if you have no greenhouse or cold frame). The seed will germinate in 10 days to 3 weeks depending on species.

As soon as the seedlings are large enough to handle, thin them out a little so they are not overcrowded, otherwise they may 'damp off' (wilt and die, because of fungal infection). They will still be closer than recommended on the packets but this is nothing to worry about.

The pots can then be moved to their permanent winter positions. They should then be treated in the same way as those potted up from the garden. Always remove leaves from the outsides of the plants so that the young leaves in the centre are allowed to develop undamaged.

Edible Flowers

You cannot have failed to notice the upsurge of 'pretty food' in recent years. Not only do our meals have to taste good, they must also look like a work of art as well. One of the easiest ways to achieve this is to scatter petals, or even whole flowers, over the dish. It is surprising how many plants can be used for this purpose, but REMEMBER, NEVER EAT ANY FLOWER UNLESS YOU KNOW THAT IT IS PERFECTLY SAFE TO DO SO. Always assume that plants are inedible unless you know that they may be eaten, otherwise you could end up with a nasty poisoning incident. NEVER LET CHILDREN EXPERIMENT WITH EATING PLANTS.

Most plants with flowers that can be eaten raw are attractive enough to plant in any sunny position in the garden – in borders, containers, baskets, or wherever. The flowers of all culinary herbs are edible, though you have to be careful where you use them since not all flower flavours go with all recipes.

Pot marigold

THE FOLLOWING ARE AMONG THE MOST USEFUL:

Anise hyssop *(Agastache anethiodora)*: the mauve-purple flowers can be chopped and dusted over salads to give a mild aniseed flavour.

Mint: the fluffy, lavender blue flower heads make a good garnish for salads and any hot or cold dish calling for the flavour of mint (eg lamb). Korean mint (*Agastache rugosa*) can be used in a similar way. The mauve flowers are similar to those of anise hyssop, but the flavour is different.

Fennel: this produces umbrella-shaped heads of many tiny, yellow flowers. If these are removed carefully with scissors, they can be scattered over fish dishes, vegetables and salads or floated on soups just before serving.

Hyssop: the white, blue, lavender or pink flowers are often used as a salad garnish.

Lavender: can be added to salads in a similar way. If the flowers are allowed to set seed, they may be incorporat ed in a wide range of cake and pudding recipes.

Rosemary: the flowers can be stripped off the stalks and used to decorate lamb or fish dishes.

Sage: the flowers are best used as a garnish for poultry or pork because of the pronounced flavour. Although it is possible to eat these flowers, the taste is rong that they are perhaps best discarded when the dish is ready to be eaten.

Savory: the individual flowers make a useful decoration for egg dishes.

Basil: if the plants are allowed to flower, the heads will brighten up and give a subtle flavour to hard-boiled egg dishes and tomatoes.

Bergamot: the aromatic, slightly orange-flavoured flowers are best used to decorate hot and cold sweets and puddings.

Borage: this is a very useful herb that produces masses of miniature, perfectly shaped, blue flowers that are easily detached from the rest of the plant. They are ideal for floating on the top of summer drinks and certain chilled soups and cold consommés.

Chives: the showy, round, lavender-pink flowers are often eaten in salads, and are an excellent garnish for any dish that can cope with a mild onion flavour. The flower heads of garlic chives may be used in a similar way, but are smaller and the off-white flowers are not so attractive.

Feverfew: this produces white, daisy-like flowers with golden centres. The petals or whole flowers can be used in salads but only in very small amounts since the flavour is pungent and not to everybody's liking.

Marjoram: mature plants of both wild and sweet marjoram produce heads of fluffy, lavender flowers that can be scattered over Italian cookery (pasta, pizza and the like).

Thyme flowers can be used similarly, or mix the two together for a subtle but clearly Mediterranean flavour.

Salad burnet: this produces curious, ball-shaped flowers that can be mixed with salad leaves to add interest.

Pot marigold: the really useful, yellow or orange petals and even whole heads may be added to salads, sprinkled over cold soups or used as a topping for green vegetables before serving.

Wild pansy (Heartsease) (right): individual flowers make an attractive finishing touch to summer cold dishes and sweets.

Sweet rocket: the pastel-coloured leaves should be sprinkled over cold puddings just before eating. Pelargonium (bedding geranium) petals are used in a similar way. The

103

petals of pelargoniums with scented leaves will impart a very faint hint of the scent of the particular pelargonium from which the petals were taken.

Nasturtium: the large, showy blooms of nasturtium are superb for adding excitement to a mixed salad. They have a subtle, slightly fragrant, slightly peppery taste that livens up the rather bland taste of lettuce and similar salad leaves considerably.

LIVING CONFECTIONERY

A delicious way to treat certain edible flowers is to crystallise or candy them. Not all flowers are suitable, the best being those with a distinctive flavour (usually those with a pronounced perfume) and a suitable shape, such as roses, sweet violets and wild pansies.

Pick roses when they are in full bloom. It is not necessary only to use deep red, heavily scented ones as most rose petals can be treated successfully in this way. Smaller flowers should be gathered when they are just mature. All flowers must be unblemished, clean and untreated with chemicals.

Holding them carefully with tweezers, dip the rose petals or whole violet flowers first into egg white beaten to the point at which it begins to stiffen and then into a small bowl of sieved icing sugar. The petals should be fully covered but not over-coated with either egg white or sugar.

Spread the dipped petals or flowers, evenly spaced and not

touching each other, on a clean, dry baking sheet and place in a warm airing cupboard for about 24 hours, or until they are crisp, dry and brittle. They can then be stored between sheets of grease-proof paper in a cool place in an airtight tin, where they should keep indefinitely if they have been properly dried. They make lovely cake decorations, or are good just to nibble as they are.

Certain herb leaves can also be crystallised, particularly mint, *agastache* and lemon balm, for use as a garnish with citrus fruits and melon. Home-made crystallised angelica always tastes better than that bought in little plastic tubs. Use stems that are not too mature, scrape the surface to remove the outer, fibrous layer and cut into pieces about 5cm (2in) long. Boil in a sugar and water solution of 285g (10oz) sugar to 570ml (1pt) water (and the pared rind of a lemon, if you like) until tender. Remove them, then coat them thoroughly with sugar. Return the stems to the sugar syrup and simmer until the liquid is clear. Place the angelica on a shallow tray and boil the syrup hard until it thickens, then pour it over the stems. Leave until they have become crystallised, then use to decorate cakes, sweets and puddings.

3

FRUIT

The Versatile Strawberry

Even if you have enough space to grow strawberries in the open ground, there are still advantages in cultivating them in containers on the patio, where they can be picked quickly, easily and cleanly without even having to take your slippers off!

Strawberries are among the most accommodating and uncomplicated plants you are ever likely to meet, and therefore lend themselves to a wide range of ornamental applications.

The main essential is to see the plants are adequately and properly fed at all times. This entails a spring top dressing of a slow-release, general-purpose fertiliser or a specific, slow-release, container plant food for pots retained for a second season, plus a weekly watering with a quick-action tomato fertiliser or flowering plant container food throughout the spring and growing season for all plantings.

STRAWBERRIES IN GROWING BAGS

This is possibly the easiest way to cultivate strawberries other than in the open ground. A standard-sized growing bag will take up to ten young plants. Cut 10cm x 10 cm (4in x 4in) holes in the top of the bag, and plant through these. Make sure that the compost is damp but not soggy, and ensure that there are plenty of drainage holes – you may need to punch these yourself.

The best time for planting is late summer and autumn, so the plants become established over the winter. However, with quick-maturing varieties like 'Temptation', you may plant module-raised seedlings right up to early summer and still expect a crop the first season.

With most varieties, late planting will give you a small yield the first season, and a normal one the next. After this, the plants should either be replanted in the garden, or discarded, but you must ensure that the bag is given the very best of care with regard to watering and feeding throughout its life.

The choice of varieties is very much a matter of personal preference, but there are two points to bear in mind. Perpetual-fruiting types produce a moderate but steady stream of fruit throughout the summer and autumn, but if you want a larger quantity all at once, it is best to opt for a variety with a single flush. To extend the strawberry season, you could always have two or more bags and choose varieties ripening at different times.

STRAWBERRIES IN POTS

The same advice applies regarding the choice of varieties when growing strawberries in pots as for raising them in growing bags. There is, however, an additional point in that, if you opt to grow strawberries in pots, you are probably looking as much at the overall ornamental value as the yield. Perpetual varieties, such as the highly recommended 'Aromel', produce pretty flowers and attractive fruit over a long period. They are therefore perhaps more suited to patio pot culture since the visual effect lasts for much longer – even into late autumn, when fruiting has finished but the leaves turn a rich orange-red.

Almost any container may be used – from expensive

TIP

If you make some holes at one end of the bag and thread through some thin polypropylene rope, you can suspend the bag as a giant hanging basket. Make sure the holes are not too near the edge, or they will tear with the weight of the bag when in full growth and the bag will fall! If you want to use your growing bag in this way, use twelve strawberry plants – six per side – and make sure that the holes are staggered so the upper plants do not smother the ones beneath them. So-called 'flower pouches' are obtainable that work on a similar principle and can be used for strawberries in much the same way, but the volume of compost is such that it cannot support many plants healthily and still produce a large crop, although the visual effect is pleasing.

stoneware to cheap plastic 'chimneys' and 'urns'. The appearance can be just as pleasing once the plants have developed. The main essential is that there should be plenty of holes in the base to prevent the compost becoming waterlogged.

The diameter and depth of the container will dictate how many strawberries you can plant – usually between five and ten. Shallow containers should only be used for one-season cropping, since the amount of compost they hold is not really adequate to support plants in the peak of condition for more than twelve months.

Again, planting should be done in late summer and autumn or at any time of the year if you want to retain your strawberry container for a second season. Later planting will produce a better crop the following year. If you do not want to replant annually, you should use a soil-based compost rather than a soil-less, general purpose one.

Place a thin layer of 20mm (three-quarter inch) gravel in the base of the container to help drainage and raise the base of the pot off the surface of the paving a little to keep the drainage holes clear. Trim back all the old foliage the second spring to tidy up the plants and give a top-dressing of a slow-release, container fertiliser. This should be used in addition to the regular feeding the container must receive throughout the growing and fruiting season.

STRAWBERRIES IN HANGING BASKETS

Growing strawberries in hanging baskets is like growing them in any other container, except that the basket is suspended in mid-air throughout its growing and fruiting life. Because of this, special care must be taken to ensure that the compost never dries out. For this reason, it is best to use John Innes No 2, although this makes the basket very heavy, so the bracket and chains must be in first-class order or you may lose the lot.

In order to cut water evaporation down to a minimum, it is best to use a solid-sided basket – the larger, the better – although I have used wire baskets, lined with polythene and then moss, quite successfully.

The maximum number of plants you can grow in a hanging basket is generally between five and eight, depending upon the diameter. Choose the deepest basket you can find, as this will hold the most compost and therefore provide the biggest (and coolest) root run.

The planting time and method is exactly the same as for any other container. After fruiting, the baskets should be removed from their brackets and over-wintered on a hard surface at ground level outdoors.

STRAWBERRIES IN WINDOW BOXES

Strawberries provide a way of filling a window box for two years without replanting that is both functional and attractive. The principle is the same as for hanging baskets, the advantage being that the containers do not wave around in the air and so are not placed under as much stress through rapid drying out.

Make sure that a window box intended for growing strawberries is deep enough to hold an adequate quantity of compost. The plants should be spaced 15–20cm (6–8in) apart.

STRAWBERRIES IN BARRELS

If you can get hold of a real wooden barrel, this is by far the best container of this sort that you are likely to find. Make round holes in the sides large enough to plant the young strawberries, but not too wide, or you will lose a lot of the compost. Around 8cm (3in) is ideal. A large barrel should be able to take about two dozen holes and you can plant another 3–5 strawberries in the top. Try not to position the holes above each other to ensure that one plant does not hang down over another.

Alternatively, purpose-made strawberry barrels are widely available, usually made of heavy-duty plastic. Similarly designed terracotta and ceramic pots – also described as 'strawberry pots' can be found, but these are generally too small to support a crop satisfactorily, although they may be used for varieties producing the best crop in the first year, like 'Temptation'. Terracotta pots dry out rapidly because of evaporation through the sides and this can affect the way the fruit develops as there is often insufficient moisture in the compost to swell the strawberries.

A good, purpose-designed, strawberry barrel has an integral, central, watering tube, down which water is poured when necessary. This ensures that all areas of the barrel receive even watering, otherwise the top can often remain dry while the compost near the base is sodden. If your barrel does not have one of these, you can easily make one by drilling small holes along the length of a piece of plastic drainpipe and inserting this in the centre of the barrel before you start to fill.

The best position for the barrel, as with all container-grown strawberries, is in full sun. Strawberries will, however, tolerate

Strawberry 'Temptation'

some morning or afternoon shade if necessary, providing this does not last for more than half the day at the height of summer and the situation is sheltered.

A full strawberry barrel, even one made of plastic, is very heavy, and you should position it where it is to live before start-ing to fill it. It should also be raised up on bricks to keep the drainage holes clear of the ground.

To plant up, first place about 2.5cm (1in) of gravel in the base to help drainage, then add compost to just above the lowest holes. You will probably find that the best medium for growing strawberries in a barrel is either half-and-half John Innes No 3 and general purpose compost, or two-thirds general purpose compost mixed with one-third John Innes No 3 if you are on a tight budget, or you think you might want to move the barrel once it is planted up. The more soil-less compost you add to the John Innes, the lighter the barrel will be, but the sooner it will need replanting.

Firm the compost gently, then introduce the first plants by pushing the roots through the holes. Top up with compost and repeat the procedure until you reach the top, and plant more strawberries to finish off the barrel. Give a good watering and then treat the strawberries in the same way as those in other con-tainers for the rest of their lives in the barrel.

Strawberries growing in a barrel in a soil-rich compost should last for about three years before the barrel has to be completely emptied and refilled with fresh compost and new plants.

GROWING STRAWBERRIES BY THE 'TABLE TOP' METHOD

This is a comparatively new method of cultivation, used at pres-ent mainly by commercial growers, in which strawberry plants are planted into growing bags or other suitable containers as already described, but these are then elevated to table-top height (about 90cm or 3ft) on structures similar to greenhouse staging. The advantage of growing strawberries in this way is that they are easier to keep an eye on – and pick, of course. The fruit is not splashed with dirty water when it rains, and slug damage is less (though not eliminated entirely, as slugs and snails will climb the legs of the supports if they want to).

You can grow quite a large number of plants in a small space by this method and if necessary you can use the area beneath the support for growing more plants, although these would need to be tolerant of the shade cast by the plants and structure above, so are more likely to be ornamental than edible.

STRAWBERRIES IN RAISED BEDS

Growing strawberries in raised beds has similar advantages to growing them by the 'table top' method. However, with this method, you would have to plant through black polythene or mulch sheeting to keep the fruit clean, as during heavy rain there is still the chance of wet compost splashing up.

The method of planting and aftercare is the same as for strawberry culture in any other type of container. Providing that the raised bed is of a reasonable size and is filled with a compost that is predominantly soil-based and the plants are always well cared-for, you should expect to get a good crop of fruit for at least three seasons and possibly a fourth.

Make sure that the raised bed is well-drained. This means leaving the mortar out of some of the vertical joints in the first course of bricks or blocks at construction time and providing about 10cm (4in) of drainage material such as broken crocks or fine brick rubble in the bottom before filling.

It is time to start again with new plants when the yield begins to dwindle in both quantity and quality. However, just as it is inadvisable to replant any fruit crop with the same type in the same soil in the open garden, you should not replace old strawberry plants with new ones in a raised bed without changing the compost completely first. If you do not feel inclined to do this, you can plant ornamental species in the same bed in the same compost and grow your patio strawberries elsewhere for the time being.

'CLIMBING STRAWBERRIES'

Many years ago, one or two unscrupulous 'plant sellers' (they could hardly be described as nurserymen) began to market very ordinary stock by means of vivid descriptions or irresistible names made up by themselves and having no connection whatever with either the correct Latin names or the common English ones.

One of these less-than-novel plants was the 'climbing strawberry'. Using imaginative artwork in weekend newspaper advertisements, this variety was endowed with amazing attributes. It was the last word in strawberry cultivation for a confined space, the 'climbing stems' being shown twining mouth-wateringly through a trellis while bearing huge crops of enormous berries.

Eventually, this marketing ploy was discouraged and the 'climbing strawberry' went the way of all dubious merchandise. What was on offer was, in fact, no different from any other strawberry variety producing long runners in great numbers (some types do this more than others). It was the runners that were described as 'climbing', whereas, in reality, they had to be trained upwards and tied into a trellis. Grown in the normal way, these runners would behave just like any others, spreading over the ground and rooting where they touched, and any strawberry runners – not just those from the so-called 'climbing strawberry' – could just as effectively be trained upwards in the same way … at a fraction of the cost!

In fact, the idea in itself is not a bad one and is certainly a method of cultivation you might like to try. For best results, the plants should be grown in the earth rather than a container, so that they have an unrestricted root run and are best planted at the edge of the patio or in a border against a wall or fence. The strawberries are planted 30cm (1ft) apart in soil and provided with a trellis or other similar, vertical means of support about 15–23cm (6–9in) away from the centre of the row.

Apple tree
'Lilliput'

The most suitable varieties are ones you would normally consider for a hanging basket or window box, with a lax habit and very long runners, such as 'Aromel', 'Guirlande' or 'Mount Kenya', though any runner-producing variety can be used if a shorter support is provided.

Plant the young strawberry plants in the normal way in late summer or autumn. The first season, a moderate crop will be produced on the main plants, followed by runners that are tied or woven into the trellis as they grow. By the end of the first season, the support should be almost covered with vertically trained runners.

In the second season, both the parent plants and those on the runners will bear fruit. The yield should be good if the plants are properly fed and watered, although the crop from the parents will be lower than if the runners had been removed because these take quite a lot of nourishment from the original plants.

The plants will continue to produce runners and, to avoid a tangle and a lot of plants at varying stages of production, it is best after cropping to remove the first runners that were produced and tie the latest ones in their place.

After about three years the yield will fall off, no matter how careful you are with feeding and training. You will have to leave the bed for at least two years before replanting with strawberries, although you could use the same trellis for other climbing edible crops in the meantime, such as peas.

Fruit in Pots and Tubs

One of the most attractive and, indeed, successful ways of growing fruit in a confined space, particularly where there is no open ground as such, is in containers. Almost all types of fruit can be cultivated in this way. The main exception is raspberries, which need some space in order to make new canes. Other types of cane fruit, like blackberries, are also possibly better dealt with in other ways because their sprawling habit needs constant attention to keep it appropriate for the small garden. Trained forms of tree fruits – cordon, fan and espalier apples, pears, plums, cherries, peaches and the like – may be planted in tubs placed against a wall, fence, trellis or similar support and tied in as if they were growing in the ground, but particular attention has to be paid to watering, because the containers are more likely to dry out when placed against a solid structure.

Container cultivation of strawberries and heathland berries is dealt with in detail on pages 117 and 118, but much larger specimens can equally well be grown in tubs using much the same techniques.

THE POT FOR THE JOB

The general rule is the larger the pot, the better. Tree fruits, even ones grafted or budded onto dwarfing rootstocks (see Appendix 3) must have very large containers eventually if they are to stay in good condition, although apples on the very dwarfing rootstock M27 will tolerate slightly smaller containers. Very young specimens may need potting first in smaller pots, then replanting in large tubs when the roots begin to emerge from the drainage holes at the bottom.

The same applies to soft fruits like gooseberries, blackcurrants, redcurrants and white currants. New plants are often very small, so may be potted on into progressively larger pots as they grow (although you may find that the less you handle gooseberry bushes, the better)!

Theoretically, the container should be as substantial as possible – preferably made of a material like wood, reconstituted stone or concrete, although there are now some excellent, heavy-

TRAINED FORMS OF FRUIT TREES

FAN

CORDON

BUSH

PYRAMID

ESPALIER

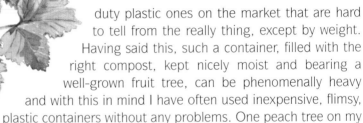

duty plastic ones on the market that are hard to tell from the really thing, except by weight. Having said this, such a container, filled with the right compost, kept nicely moist and bearing a well-grown fruit tree, can be phenomenally heavy and with this in mind I have often used inexpensive, flimsy, plastic containers without any problems. One peach tree on my patio has been in such a pot for the last ten years without ill-effects and has produced a better crop every year. It now requires repotting but only because the plastic has begun to crack.

The vital point is that the tub should be well-drained. One central drainage hole is usually adequate, as long as it is large enough. Alternatively, several smaller ones dispersed evenly across the base are acceptable. If your chosen tub has no drainage holes, you will have to drill some before proceeding any further (see left).

POTTING UP

Use a good, soil-based, potting compost, such as John Innes No 3. If you think you may want to move the tub regularly, you can lighten its weight by mixing in thoroughly up to one-quarter of perlite (an inert, lightweight, granular volcanic material), which will make the tub a little lighter without destroying the structure and beneficial properties of the soil-based compost.

It is a good idea to fill the tub *in situ*, to avoid having to carry a very heavy container to its chosen location. As the base should be raised off the paving or earth to prevent the drainage holes gradually becoming blocked, the pot feet (or whatever you use to lift it) should be in position before starting to fill with compost.

Start to fill the pot by placing about 8cm (3in) of drainage material – coarse gravel, broken crocks, crushed bricks or crumbled polystyrene packing blocks – in the bottom. Add a layer of compost just deep enough to allow you to place the roots of the new fruit tree in the container at the correct depth to ensure that, when you finish filling, the tree is planted no more or less deeply than it was before.

This will help you, among other things, not to bury any budding or grafting union (this looks like a knob or kink in the stem, usually a few inches above ground level), which would reduce the effectiveness – generally dwarfing – of the rootstock. In fact, burying the union is not as serious when the tree is pot-grown as when it is planted in the open ground, as the constricting effect of the container will eventually cause growth to slow. However, even so, it is better not to.

Top up with more compost, firming gently as you do so, until within about 5cm (2in) of the rim of the tub. Water well until it runs out of the drainage holes. This will make sure that the compost is evenly moist and properly settled. You may find that, having done this, you need to top up again, particularly if you have added perlite to the original compost.

You can finish off by covering the top of the compost with gravel or ornamental chippings, if you wish. This is not essential, but creates a good effect, helps to conserve moisture in the tub and also reduces the growth of weeds, moss and algae on the surface.

AFTERCARE

Fruit trees in containers should last without the need for disturbance for many years if potted up correctly at the outset. The main essential is regular and even watering, especially after the young fruit has begun to swell.

There will be enough fertiliser in the compost to get the trees and bushes off to a good start, after which time, you will need to give a supplementary feed. This should consist of an annual top-dressing of a dry powder or granular, slow release fertiliser (according to the manufacturer's instructions) in February, boosted with a weekly liquid feed of a tomato- or similar fertiliser from late spring to early autumn.

SPECIAL POINTS RELATING TO INDIVIDUAL TYPES OF FRUIT

APPLES AND PEARS

Tub cultivation is a good way of growing the very narrow, tall ballerina apples that, planted in the open ground, often grow so high that they become ungainly and the fruit at the top is impossible to pick. Restricting the roots by growing in containers will curtail growth a good deal after the first year or so. 'Minarette' and pillarette apples will also grow successfully in tubs, but their pole-like shape is not the most attractive for such features. The design aspect may be improved by planting bedding plants in the compost at the base of the trees, in which case, you should omit covering it with chippings when planting up.

The best forms for tub cultivation as far as appearance is con-

cerned are bushes and dwarf pyramids. Little pruning is required if well-trained trees were used in the first place and mainly consists of removing badly placed shoots as they appear, to keep a good shape. This can be done from late summer onwards. There is no need to prune to encourage fruit formation; the influence of the rootstock and the restrictive effect of the tub will see to this.

PLUMS, GAGES AND CHERRIES

Again, bush forms are the most pleasing for ornamental container cultivation. As in the open ground, pruning should be kept to a minimum and should be confined to thinning the head out to prevent overcrowding. This must be done during warmer weather after the crop has been picked, to avoid infection by the low-temperature fungal disease, silver leaf.

Plums and cherries grown in containers will usually start bearing good crops earlier than their counterparts planted in the open ground.

PEACHES, NECTARINES AND APRICOTS

These are ideal for patio cultivation, and in recent years, some excellent new varieties, many with large, ornamental or coloured leaves, have been introduced for use in this kind of situation. Apricots are always more difficult to grow outdoors in Great Britain and should be given the sunniest, most sheltered spot on the patio.

Pruning is rarely necessary when this type of fruit is container-grown and is usually limited to the removal of dead, dying and weak wood and overcrowded and badly placed shoots, in order to establish and maintain a well-shaped, healthy head.

FIGS

If you want good crops of figs early in the life of the plant, pot cultivation is a must. Most young fig trees have had some preliminary training to start establishing the traditional fan shape for wall cultivation. Try to find one that has not already received this treatment so the head has remained bushy. Any pruning will only be needed during the first year or so, to create well-spaced branches for a nicely shaped head. The roots will soon fill the container, after which time regular pruning should no longer be necessary.

Pear Tree
'Concorde'

Dwarf peach tree
(opposite)

116

BLACKCURRANTS

Prune by removing about one-third of the shoots every year at the base. This will ensure that the bush is kept young and neat and continues to crop well.

GOOSEBERRIES, REDCURRANTS AND WHITE CURRANTS

Pot-grown gooseberries and similar types of soft fruit are effective and equally productive either grown as a bush on a short, single leg (as they should be when you buy them), or trained as a short standard.

Prune after picking the crop by cutting back the side shoots that have borne fruit to five leaves and cut back again to two dormant buds from the main branches in early winter. Shorten the leader (the top of the main shoot) in winter by one-third until the bush has reached the size you want it, then treat as the side shoots.

RHUBARB

No stems should be pulled the first season after planting and only a few the next season. To maintain vigour, try not to remove too many stems from any one tub, even when the plant is established. Pot-grown rhubarb should be removed from the container and divided after about four years or when vigour starts to diminish. To ensure a regular supply, you should therefore have several pots of different ages on the go at the same time.

Gooseberry 'Rolunda'

Hanging Fruit Gardens

GROWING FRUIT IN HANGING BASKETS AND WINDOW BOXES

Because most fruit is produced on comparatively large plants, the choice of subjects for hanging baskets and window boxes is somewhat limited. It is, however, possible to grow certain types successfully and, fortunately, these happen to be some of the most ornamental forms. They are therefore not only productive, but can also provide an attractive feature.

The obvious choice of fruit for containers of this sort is the **strawberry** and in the first section of this part on fruit you can

Strawberry 'Aromel'

discover what a thoroughly good plant this is for ornamental baskets and boxes.

Heathland berries are, however, just as practical and fun to grow as edible basket plants, providing varieties with a suitable habit are chosen. The important thing to remember before you start is that all these berries are lime-haters and that their natural environment is similar to that of those heathers that flower in summer (those flowering in winter – mainly varieties of *Erica carnea* and *E. x darleyensis* – will tolerate lime). Hence the generic description 'heathland' berries.

There are many areas in which these acid-loving fruit bushes will not grow successfully since the soil contains more lime than they can tolerate. Because of this, they are eminently suitable for container cultivation since they can then be provided with exactly the right aspect and medium for them to thrive.

HOW TO START

First, look for the right varieties. High-bush blueberries are not suitable because they eventually make large bushes and hard pruning will affect the crop. Always choose low-bush blueberries. These are the ones you see growing with heather on the moors and have a low, spreading habit.

For an even better visual effect, try the cranberry, a prostrate, evergreen, ericaceous shrub that produces the tasty red berries so popular for serving with turkey as a sauce or jelly. The fruit ripens in September or October depending on locality so, if you want cranberries for Christmas, you will need to pick them when just ripe and freeze them.

THE COMPOST

To grow heathland berries successfully, they should be planted in a compost with a pH of around 4, which is very acid. Using a ready-made ericaceous compost is the easiest answer. However, as, correctly planted and in the right size of container, they will carry on happily for several years without replanting, it is advisable to use a compost that is slightly more substantial. This can be achieved by adding a quarter by volume of good garden soil to a proprietary ericaceous compost.

You will need to check the pH of the mixture after adding the soil. If it has been raised much above four, you will also need to incorporate some flowers of sulphur (available from the sundries section of the garden centre) to bring it down again. Follow the instructions accompanying the container.

THE BASKET OR BOX

You should use a solid-sided basket since the compost will dry out far too much for good fruit production in a wire one. Choose as large a one as possible.

A window box should be deep enough to provide a good root run and, for the best visual effect, as wide and long as is possible. To look pleasing as well as being productive, you need a good number of plants per container. Heathland berries must have a cool root run so the walls of the basket or box should be as thick and substantial as you can find.

This kind of fruit will tolerate some shade, providing it is not dense and total, so they may be given a north-east or north-west aspect.

PLANTING UP

Use about three plants per hanging basket, according to the diameter of the basket. In a window box, the plants should be spaced about 20cm (8in) apart. In a wide box, they may be planted in two staggered rows, one at the front of the box, the other at the back, with about 15cm (6in) between plants.

AFTERCARE

Always use soft water if available. Regular watering with hard water will gradually increase the pH of the soil to a point where the plants can no longer grow healthily. This means that, if you live in a hard water area, it is inadvisable to use automatic watering straight off the mains supply.

If you do not have access to rainwater, remember that water produced by defrosting the refrigerator or freezer is also soft, as is that from a dehumidifier. If all else fails, use cooled, boiled water, which contains less lime, but watch the plants carefully for any signs of yellowing or poor growth and treat with sequestrene or an ericaceous plant tonic immediately.

Never allow the compost to become at all dry. This means checking it constantly in hot, dry weather, particularly after the first year, when the container will be very full of roots. Feed with a specific ericaceous plant food, according to the manufacturer's instructions, throughout the growing season.

Pruning usually only consists of a gentle clipping to keep the bushes in shape. They are of naturally dwarf habit, so should never get too large for their situation.

Fruit as Ornamental Wall Shrubs

Some edible plants require a degree of imagination to fit them attractively into an ornamental situation. This is not the case with many kinds of fruit, however, which not only combine well with all types of solely decorative plants but may often outstrip them in the interest they can provide.

This is particularly true of the sorts of fruit that can be grown on walls and fences. These generally have a pleasing form, delightful flowers and top off the whole show with large crops of attractive and delicious fruit.

PRUDENT PLANTING

THE SUPPORT

For maximum success with any type of fruit trained on a wall or fence, good planting is essential. In order that you can train your

Fan-trained family
apple tree

specimens exactly where you want them to grow and at exactly
the right time, it is advisable to provide adequate supports first.
These may be as simple or elaborate as you wish, from a framework of strong, galvanised wires stretched horizontally at
30–38cm (12–15in) spacings, to trelliswork so ornamental that
it could almost be a feature on its own. If you do not put up the
supports before planting, training will invariably be neglected and
can more often than not end up as emergency nails knocked in
all over the wall or fence when the tree starts to flop – a practice
that is good neither for the plant nor the wall!

THE SOIL

To keep wall fruit at the peak of condition, the soil it is planted in
should be of really good quality, containing plenty of organic
material to help to conserve moisture, which may be scarce at the
base of a solid structure.

Although it is possible to grow trained fruit in large containers, you will generally get much better results if it is planted in the open ground. On a patio this will often necessitate lifting paving slabs or removing a piece of concrete unless holes were specifically left for wall plants when the feature was laid. The planting area should not be less than 60cm square and 60cm deep (2ft square and 2ft deep), to allow for replacing the sand, rubble and subsoil beneath with sufficient decent topsoil, or, if this is not available, John Innes No 3 compost.

PLANTING

The technique for planting wall-trained fruit is exactly the same as for open-grown plants. Planting depth should be not less or more than in the container or nursery bed and, if the tree was grafted (this usually only applies to 'top fruit', such as apples, pears, plums, peaches), the union between the variety and the rootstock must be well above the soil surface.

Add a couple of handfuls of bone meal to the soil as you refill the hole, if planting in the autumn, or a slow-release general-purpose fertiliser in spring.

Water the new specimen in very well and check regularly to make sure the soil is always moist for at least the first two years after planting. Sunny walls are very hot and the soil at the base dries out rapidly, even in spring and autumn. Remember, too, that rain will only reach this area when the wind is blowing towards the wall so, even during a wet spell, the roots of a wall-trained plant may remain unacceptably dry.

Apple blossom

BASIC TRAINING

Start foundation training as soon as the specimen has been plant-ed by tying it in to the support in the shape you wish it to follow.

PRETTY FRUIT FOR PRETTY WALLS

Possibly the most striking fruit to double as ornamental wall plants are those types that normally grow as trees or large bush-es – that is, apples, pears, plums, gages, cherries, peaches, nec-tarines and apricots.

Apples and pears for this kind of cultivation are usually trained as espaliers, although fan-trained forms are available. Espaliers and fans usually take up quite a lot of space (up to 4m or 12ft width), although better specialist fruit nurseries offer a choice of trained fruit grafted onto a variety of dwarfing, semi-dwarfing and very dwarfing rootstocks to fit various wall or fence areas. However, if your favourite apple or pear is not self-fertile, or if you want more than one kind, you will probably have to invest in a family fruit tree, where two or three different kinds which pollinate each other are grafted onto the same stock. This will be more expensive, but less so than buying two or three dif-ferent plants and will probably provide you with as much fruit as you need of each individual variety anyway.

Unfortunately, it is not possible to graft apples and pears onto the same stock, so if you want both, you need to plant a speci-men of each.

Plums and cherries are generally trained as fans and, grown as such, produce a colossal amount of fruit. To get the best out of wall-trained apples, pears and plums, they should be given a

Dwarf nectarine

CORDON

ESPALIER

sunny aspect. This is also true of sweet cherries, but acid cherries such as Morello will thrive on a totally sunless wall or fence.

Peaches and nectarines often produce much larger and better crops when trained on sunny walls and fences. In Britain, this is the only reliable way to grow apricots, which really need a warmer climate than our own to produce decent crops of good-quality fruit.

Because of their growth habit and the way they form their fruit, **plums, cherries, peaches, nectarines and apricots** for wall cultivation are, as a rule, only available as fans or very young trees suitable for training as such.

Trained tree fruits will reliably produce more flower clusters and heavier crops than their open-grown counterparts. They look magnificent when in full blossom and again when the branches are laden with swelling fruit in late summer and autumn.

PRUNING TREE FRUITS

Once the shape of the tree (espalier or fan) has been established, pruning is a straightforward and pleasant job and can be done in early autumn. **Apples and pear** espaliers and fans are pruned by cutting back the sub-lateral shoots produced on the lateral branches to 3–4 buds (see left). Fruiting spurs will then be produced on these. Shoots subsequently arising from the sub-laterals are shortened back to one bud in the same way.

Any diseased, dying or unwanted mature wood can be cut out during winter since it is easier to assess the shape and state of the tree when the branches are bare.

Plums and cherries are treated in a similar way, pinching out unwanted young shoots in early summer to leave 6 leaves and shortening them by a half in early autumn after harvesting. When shoots that are required to form the fan-shape and fill wall space have reached the required length, they too should be pinched out. The removal of any mature wood should be done in spring to prevent infection with silver leaf disease.

Peaches, nectarines and the like are rather more complicated. Any shoots growing directly outwards or towards the wall should be rubbed out in spring. At the same time, the young growth buds on each flowering lateral are pinched out to leave three buds. In May, each shoot arising from these is cut back to 6 leaves. After picking the fruit, the fruited laterals are cut out and replaced with the young lateral produced from the lowest of the three buds left when pruning in spring.

To reduce infection from peach leaf curl (a debilitating and unsightly disease in which the leaves of peaches and related species become distorted, blistered and turn red), it is advisable to keep the tree dry with an open-sided shelter of clear polythene from December to May, when the disease, which can be carried on rain, is at its most infectious.

The alternative to tree fruits is to use the kinds of cane fruit that lend themselves to ornamental training – mainly **blackberries** and their hybrid relations **boysenberries, tayberries, loganberries** and the like.

For optimum appearance, those varieties with decorative leaves, preferably evergreen and ideally thornless, like the 'Oregon Thornless' blackberry, should be planted, but varieties fitting these criteria are scarce and, in general, the flavour and quality of the fruit is rather inferior. The best variety to choose is therefore the one that suits the palate best. You can maximise decorative appeal by careful and regular training.

In its most basic form, training consists of training the young canes fan-wise, leaving some space in the middle. The new canes, produced over the summer, are tied in together in this space to keep them tidy. After harvesting, the old canes, which usually die anyway, are removed completely and the ones bunched together in the middle are untied and retrained to replace those that have been cut out.

FIGS

Figs have some of the most spectacular leaves of any wall shrub suitable for growing in a temperate climate and are therefore worth cultivating for the foliage alone, the fruit being an additional bonus. On a south- or west-facing wall, once the tree has reached a certain degree of maturity, ripe figs should be obtained in all but the worst seasons.

Young fig trees are usually sold with two branches, partially trained to develop into a fan, but they are expensive and, as they grow quickly at this stage, it will save you money (and give you satisfaction) to produce your own from a small, single-stemmed specimen. These may be found at some smaller nurseries. Once planted, side shoots will soon be produced and these can be retained and tied in, or removed as necessary.

Figs growing on a root system that is allowed to develop unchecked will become absolutely enormous in a very short time, so it is vital that at planting time some measures are taken to curtail root growth to a large extent. The best way to do this is dig out a cube of soil with 60cm (2ft) sides and line the hole with paving slabs placed on edge. The bottom should contain about 30cm (1ft) of well-rammed brick or concrete rubble to act as a barrier between the strong taproot and the soil underneath while still providing adequate drainage. The fig is planted in good quality soil in this pit, which is, in effect, a sunken container. Growth will slow up when the roots fill the space within the vertical slabs and while some roots will eventually penetrate the barrier at the corners, the resultant tree will usually be considerably smaller than if left to its own devices.

The fruit is produced in a unique way. Embryo figs are produced without pollination in autumn and these swell into mature fruits the following summer. Baby figs produced too early in the season are unlikely to reach maturity as they are usually damaged in the winter and are aborted the next spring. In the coldest parts of the United Kingdom, it is a good idea to protect the embryonic fruit with horticultural fleece during very inclement weather in winter and early spring. However, the varieties sold for cultivation in this country are very hardy, and in most parts should need no protection at all if planted against a warm wall or fence.

Once the main branch framework of the wall-trained fig has been established, it is advisable to keep pruning to the minimum required to maintain a good fan or espalier shape. Any pruning is best carried out in very early spring, before the sap starts to rise, as the tree will bleed copiously from any cut made during the growing season and this, in theory though rarely in practice, can weaken the tree. The white latex produced is also highly irritant to the skins of some people. (It produces big blisters on my skin that take many weeks to heal, so I am always careful to cover up properly whenever I have to do any work on my own fig.)

The ornamental value of grapevines is on a par with that of figs. The leaves are attractively shaped, colouring up well in autumn, and the insignificant flowers of most varieties have a delicate and delicious fragrance when produced in sufficient quantities.

GRAPES

Grapevines whose sole function in life is fruit production have very exacting demands of cultivation and training. However, the main function of those trained on a garden fence or house wall is a decorative appearance and training and pruning are therefore a secondary consideration.

In this case, they can be treated very much like any ornamental vine or other true climbing plant when used for a wall or fence. Provide a strong trellis support over the whole of the area you want the grapevine to cover and tie the main shoots in where you want them to form a framework (grapevines produce tendrils so it is only necessary to do this to the growths that will eventually make the structure of the plant). Once you have a good coverage, you need only remove unwanted stems in late winter as and when necessary.

KIWI FRUIT

Kiwi plants are highly ornamental, with bold, heart-shaped, slightly furry leaves, hairy stems, large, fragrant, cream-coloured flowers and fruit on female plants that is both striking to look at and delicious to eat.

Kiwi plants take up a lot of space, and as two (male and female) are generally required to produce a crop, you need a big wall or plenty of wall space if they are not to become a nuisance. The alternative is to grow the miniature, self-fertile form 'Issai'. The fruits are smaller but they do not require peeling so they are ideal for the busy cook.

Kiwi fruit plants are treated in much the same way as grapes, so training and pruning outdoors can be restricted to tying in where required and removing excessive growth. It is a plant that should be grown as much for its appearance as its crop, and therefore its visual effect, if planted in a prominent position, is the main priority.

Fruiting Screens

Trained fruit bushes are one of the best ways of dividing or screening areas of the garden, but they are particularly effective in a patio situation, providing not only privacy and shelter but also the convenience of fruit on the doorstep, without even needing to remove your carpet slippers, should you so desire!

STURDY SUPPORTS

A fruit screen is a long-term feature. Many subjects will live a long time if properly planted, trained, pruned and regularly cared for and so it is vital to provide a sturdy support from the outset –

even before starting to plant. Suggestions for supports can be found in The Two Metres by One Metre Fruit Garden. The only types of screening fruit suitable for the patio that do not require a substantial framework those trained as minarettes and pillarettes and Ballerina apples. These may be planted as close together as 80cm (30in) and, although they should not be allowed to put on so much growth that they touch, will successfully act as a barrier in most situations.

TREE FRUITS AS SCREENS

S-system of tree fruit training

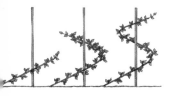

Espalier or fan-trained apples, pears, plums, gages, cherries, peaches and nectarines, are ideal screening subjects. As most will require spacing no less than 3–5m (10–15ft) apart depending on the degree of dwarfing effect of the rootstock, you are unlikely to need more than one or two to provide an efficient screen.

If you are looking for variety, you will therefore need to plant a family apple or pear tree. However, if plums, cherries or peaches are more what you have in mind, you will have to make do with one good species of each per tree.

V-system of tree fruit training

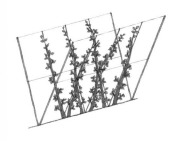

The alternative is to use cordons. Single cordons and minarettes (pillarettes) are basically the same, but single cordons are usually set at an angle of 45° and tied into a framework, whereas 'minarettes' and the like generally require no support or just a short stake at the base to prevent the young tree from rocking about excessively in high winds while it establishes itself.

Double and multiple cordons have two or more vertical main arms growing from the main trunk. They occupy slightly less space than a row of single cordons, but, like espaliers and fans, variety is limited, and training and pruning are more complicated.

A comparatively new method of training is the 'S' system (see left). This is done by bending a single-stemmed cordon around a pole or on a trellis in an S-shape. By breaking the upward sap flow, large crops are produced in a short time. Each tree requires a 2m (6ft) spacing, and should produce around 8–10 kg (20lb) of fruit in 5 years.

Another new way of training, to provide a heavy overall crop of a lot of different types of apples or pears in a short row, is the 'V' system (see left). Cordon plants are spaced about 45cm (18in) apart and trained on a V-framework of posts and wires (see illustration). When mature, a 2m (6ft) row of heavy-cropping varieties can produce around 20–25kg (50lbs) of fruit.

If you are looking not so much for privacy, but for a positive, attractive and productive edge to the patio, or even a flower bed or vegetable plot, then the stepover is an option. This is, in essence, a one-tiered espalier apple or pear that is trained on a single wire support at a height at which you can step over it. In all respects, it is treated like a normal espalier-trained fruit tree.

Stepover apples

SELF-SUPPORTING SCREENS

The most effective and pleasing fruit screen is one where the fruit is formally and artistically trained on a framework of wires or strong trellis. However, there may be occasions where it is not possible to provide this support and this is where, if you particularly want 'top fruits' like apples, pears and plums, you will need to plant pillarette-type trained forms, or Ballerina apples.

Pillarettes are suitable for most situations of this sort, but Ballerina apples need using with care. Unlike pillarettes, which are produced from normal varieties of tree fruits with a conventional growth habit, Ballerinas have been bred from a naturally-occurring mutation in which an apple was found to produce fruiting spurs directly off a main trunk, rather than on side branches, as is usually the case.

At present, the number of varieties of Ballerinas is limited, and the flavour is considered by many to be, in general, inferior to that of our favourite 'normal' varieties. There are other drawbacks, too. They are often prone to the disease apple canker, which causes dead areas in the bark. If this completely encircles the trunk, which is often the case, then that part of the tree above the lesion will die. Canker in its early stages can be treated by cutting out the affected wood and painting the area with a proprietary tree wound paint, but it is far better to plant canker-resistant varieties in the first place.

Another 'minus' is the fact that although Ballerinas are claimed to be branchless, they do actually produce short, stubby branches as they mature, which can be quite unsightly. Cut them off and more of the same habit and appearance will be produced. However, by far the most annoying feature of Ballerinas is the height to which they can eventually grow. In my garden I have three which, over the last fourteen or so years, have reached more than 5–6m (17ft). In their defence, they are the varieties that are apparently resistant to canker, and therefore produce regular, prodigious amounts of fruit. Unfortunately, the top ones are virtually impossible to pick! If you shorten back the tree, it will start to bush out and will end up looking much like an ordinary apple tree, only more ugly.

CANE FRUITS

Just as it is quite acceptable to use cane fruits such as blackberries, loganberries, tayberries and other hybrid berries as decorative wall plants, so they can also be considered as a functional and equally aesthetic alternative to conventional ornamental climbers for patio screen. These can be treated in the same way as on page 124 (Fruit as Ornamental Wall Shrubs).

However, it is also possible to use raspberries for this purpose. Plant single canes of virus-free certified stock, spaced 45cm (18in) apart, preferably in October or November or alternatively in early spring. Cut the new canes to 30cm (1ft) above ground level at planting time if this was not already done by the nursery, then cut the canes back again to just above ground level when new shoots begin to appear around the existing canes. Tie these new growths in to the supports as they grow.

BUSH FRUIT

Cordon-trained gooseberries, white currants and red currants can be used around the patio as dwarf screens. Trained gooseberry bushes are available as single, double and triple cordons from specialist fruit nurseries and will establish best if planted in autumn, although container-grown bushes may be planted at other times of the year if the weather is favourable (not during periods of heavy frost or drought).

Single cordon gooseberries should be spaced 30–38cm (12–15in) apart. You should allow about 60cm (2ft) between double cordons and 90cm (3ft) between triple cordon plants.

Unlike single cordon tree fruits, single cordon gooseberries and red and white currants are usually allowed to grow vertically. The arms of the cordons are tied to canes that are themselves tied to the main wire or trellis supports.

Because of their growth and fruiting habit, it is not possible to train blackcurrants as cordons.

MISCELLANEOUS FRUIT
(figs, grapes, kiwi fruit)

These are dealt with at length on the section on Fruit as Ornamental Wall Shrubs. Their cultivation as screening plants is virtually identical, the only real difference being that, in theory, fruit can be picked from both sides if the support. However, most of the crop will usually be found on the sunniest side.

TRAINING AND PRUNING

TREE FRUITS

The training of espaliers and fans is dealt with in Fruit as Ornamental Wall Shrubs, pages 124-5.

Cordon apples and pears are pruned in early autumn by shortening back the leader by about one-third to a well-placed bud (the junction between a leaf and the stem usually contains a dormant bud, even if it is too small to see). As the length of the cordon grows, it can be retrained on the support at a more acute angle to allow more of the stem to be tied to the framework.

Any side shoots longer than 15cm (6in) should be shortened to 3 or 4 buds beyond the fruit spurs at the base. The basic training of minarettes and pillarettes is the same.

Cordon plums, gages, damsons and cherries (and minarettes and pillarettes) are pruned in spring in a similar way.

Because of their growth habit, you are unlikely to find cordon versions of peaches and nectarines.

BUSH FRUITS

Cordon red and white currants and gooseberries are pruned in summer (preferably late June) and late winter. Shorten the side shoots to five leaves and tie the leader into the cane in summer, then shorten the side shoots again to one or two buds in winter.

The leader is shortened back by about one-third each winter until it has reached the required length, after which it is treated in the same way as the side shoots.

CANE FRUITS

The training and pruning of blackberries and hybrid berries is dealt with on pages 124-5. Summer-fruiting raspberries should have the old, fruited canes removed immediately after the berries have been picked. The new canes that will be produced from the base over the rest of summer can be tied into the wires or trellis as they grow. When growth has ceased in autumn, the tops of any particularly tall canes can be made neater by cutting back to the top of the support or just above the top wire.

Autumn-fruiting raspberry varieties should be cut to the ground completely in late autumn or winter.

MISCELLANEOUS FRUITS

The training and pruning of figs, grapes and kiwi fruits is dealt with on pages 125-127.

PLANTING TIPS

To get maximum crops, the young fruit trees and bushes must receive the best possible care when planting. Dig over the soil thoroughly to a depth of 40cm (15in) and incorporate plenty of well-rotted manure.

If planting in autumn and winter, mix 2–3 handfuls of bone-meal in with the soil when back-filling. When planting at other times of the year, mix in a balanced, slow-release fertiliser according to the manufacturer's instructions.

Make sure that you have dug a big enough hole to accommodate the roots or root ball comfortably. Place the plant in the hole at the same depth as it was growing in the nursery bed or container. Never cover the budding or grafting union of a fruit tree with soil or the effects of the rootstock will be lost. Fruit trees are grafted on to special stocks to slow up growth and ensure early cropping.

Firm the compost gently but firmly when back-filling so that the newly planted tree or bush cannot be pulled out again if you give it a gentle tug. Tie the new fruit tree or bush to its support immediately after planting. Give the roots a good soaking, and make sure it never dries out while it is establishing itself.

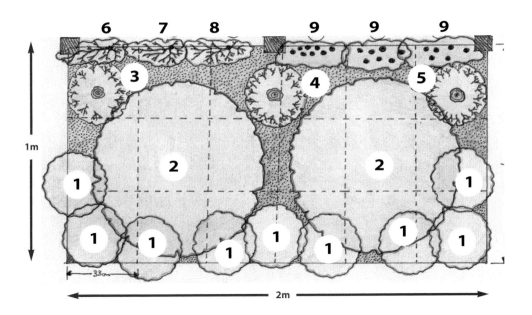

1 Strawberries 'Temptation'	6 Cordon Gooseberry 'Invicta'
2 Blackcurrents 'Ben Sarek'	7 Cordon Gooseberry 'Jubilee'
3 Minarette apple 'Falstaff'	8 Cordon Gooseberry
4 Minarette pear 'Concorde'	'Whitesmith'
5 Minarette plum 'Victoria'	9 Raspberries 'Glen Moy'

The Two Metres by One Metre Fruit Garden

With modern fruit varieties, training methods and propagation techniques, it is possible to have the miniature equivalent of a full-sized orchard in an area of two square metres (a little over two square yards). Although the planting scheme shown here is intended for the edge of a patio or similar area, there is no reason why it should not be used elsewhere in any garden, large or small, if you are not looking for huge amounts of any particular types of fruit.

DESIGN CONSIDERATIONS

This mini-fruit garden can be used either as a border at the side of a paved area or lawn, or as an island bed, surrounded by paving or grass. To maximise the very limited space, however, it is best that the design should be viewed from one side only, the side furthest away from the viewer being the one where supports are provided for formally trained bushes or those with a lax habit. Ideally, this support should be free-standing (see plan on page 133) to enable you to access the plants for maintenance and fruit picking. The simplest free-standing support comprises three 10cm x 10 cm (4in x 4in) wooden posts, pressure-treated with a plant-friendly preservative, on to which tautly stretched, heavy-duty, galvanised wire is tacked at 30cm (1ft) horizontal spacings. The height of the support should be about 2m (6ft), which means that the posts need to be 2.3m (7ft 6in) long. This allows for sufficient depth of timber underground to make the structure stable. Alternatively, the posts can be fixed into the soil with post anchors, in which case they will only need to be the nominal 2m (6ft) long. Do not sink the posts in concrete as this encourages rapid rotting at ground level.

If you want something rather more elaborate, you can use strong trellis instead of galvanised wires, or, if funds run to it and the effect is appropriate, wrought iron screening is another possibility.

Another option is to use an existing timber fence or wall as the back support. However, remember that, because in this case you cannot get round the support to access the bushes and pick the fruit, you will need to allow extra room in front of the back row. This means that, although the actual space the fruit plants occupy is still the same, the depth of the border will be greater than one metre.

CHOOSING VARIETIES

Obviously, the main consideration is what fruits you and your family prefer. In the suggested layout (page 133), I have included strawberries, blackcurrants, apples, pears, plums, gooseberries and raspberries, because this is what I felt the average person was likely to want. However, if, for example, you do not like gooseberries and raspberries, then a compact form of blackberry or hybrid berry could be planted instead. Or if you like raspberries a lot but can take or leave gooseberries, you could leave these out and use the whole of the two metre long support for raspberry canes.

On the other hand, if you like one particular gooseberry above all others, there is no need to grow cordons of three different varieties. Similarly, you do not have to grow apples, pears and plums if you only like, say, apples. Different types of tree fruit like these will not pollinate each other, so one specific sort is not essential for the well-being of another. The example shown is merely an indication of just how many kinds of fruit can be grown in a very small space, given the right varieties in the best forms and some careful planning.

Before any planting is done, it is vital that the scheme is drawn out accurately to scale – you will find it helpful if you use graph paper. It is not enough to buy the plants and just place them in the bed. Most of them will be very small and it is easy to over-plant and not allow enough room between individual specimens, particularly as spacings vary widely, from a few centimetres for strawberries to more than a metre for blackcurrants.

RASPBERRIES

Choose raspberry varieties for their flavour and the amount of fruit they produce, rather than how long they continue to crop. Raspberries freeze well and any surplus can be stored in this way. The variety 'Glen Moy' in the example has both these attributes, with the added bonus of a compact habit, some resistance to greenfly infestation and canes without prickles, making it eminently suitable for this application. Another 'plus' is its ability to produce a second, smaller crop on the new canes in the autumn before the main crop the following summer.

You will only need to plant three canes initially. This will seem a bit meagre at the outset but, after the first season, they will start making substantial stools (clumps), with several canes per stool. For pruning, see page 125.

Other compact cane fruits that could be considered instead of raspberries are the thornless blackberries 'Loch Ness', 'Veronique' and 'Waldo' and the Japanese wineberry. In this case, one plant would occupy the whole of the back row. For training, see page 130.

GOOSEBERRIES

To maximise yield and facilitate picking, you should grow cordon-trained bushes in this kind of situation. If you want smaller quantities of two or three different varieties, you will need single cordons. There is not enough space in the illustrated example for double or triple cordons unless you only want one sort.

The recommended varieties 'Invicta', 'Jubilee' and 'Whitesmith' are all good varieties for modern gardens ... heavy cropping with an excellent flavour and good disease resistance. For pruning, see page 117.

Redcurrants and white currants have a similar habit to gooseberries and can therefore be included as well as, or instead of, them. For the best yield, flavour, disease resistance and visual effect, try the redcurrant 'Jonkheer van Tets', and/or the comparatively new white currant 'Rovada'.

Gooseberries, redcurrants and white currants, trained on a single stem as short standards, may be substituted for the two blackcurrant bushes in the example. In this case, providing they are regularly pruned, you will have room for three. These can be under-planted with more strawberries if desired.

BLACKCURRANTS

This is the one type of soft fruit that is difficult to integrate into a project of this kind. Because blackcurrants have a different fruiting habit from redcurrants, gooseberries and white currants, they cannot be grown in a trained form. Conventional pruning consists of removing entirely some of the oldest branches every year to promote the production of strong, new shoots from ground level, so as the bushes mature, they can become very wide-spreading. Most blackcurrant varieties make large bushes anyway, so the number you can incorporate is restricted to one or two and you may decide that the area they occupy could be put to better use.

However, by planting the compact variety 'Ben Sarek' and using a different method of pruning, you can have blackcurrants in your mini-orchard on smaller bushes, and get a good crop.

Blackcurrants are borne on wood produced the previous season. This pruning method comprises growing two bushes and cutting one entirely to ground level every other year. The unpruned bush provides the crop. This is then cut hard back immediately after fruiting (to make fruit picking easier, you can remove the branches with the fruit still on them and strip off the berries at a more convenient height, thus pruning and gathering as a single job!). Meanwhile, the shoots on the other bush, which were produced after pruning in a similar way the previous year, are maturing and ripening, to produce the blackcurrant crop for the following season.

TREE FRUIT: APPLES, PEARS AND PLUMS

It is possible to use miniature apple trees in a project of this sort, provided they are budded or grafted onto the very dwarfing M27 rootstock, but there is no pear or plum rootstock that does quite the same job so, if you want as wide a selection of this kind of fruit as possible, you would do better to look for specimens specially trained to grow in a compact and vertical manner. The most widely known of these is the minarette or pillarette, which is, in essence, a single cordon (a fruit tree trained and pruned to crop on a single, main trunk) that is grown vertically instead of at an angle (see page 113 for more on cordons).

Single fruit of pot-grown minarette apple 'Howgate Wonder'

A bed of this size will accommodate three pillarette fruit trees if all the other recommended kinds of fruits are included as well. Of course, if you so wish, you could give the whole area over to tree fruits, in which case you could have up to ten pillarettes; under-planted with strawberries. This is another option with which you could impress your fellow gardening friends!

If you intend to go for diversity, all the varieties must be self-fertile. Minarettes and pillarettes are not available from every garden centre, so you may have to buy them mail order from a specialist fruit nursery. The best of these should be able to offer you self-fertile varieties of a wide range of tree fruits – apples, pears, plums, gages and damsons – so you should be able to find what you are looking for, though it may take a little time.

Another alternative is to plant a fan-trained or espalier fruit tree, or conventional, single cordons, on the back support instead of the cane fruit bushes. This length will take up to seven single cordons, but only one fan or espalier. A family fruit tree (one where several different but compatible varieties have been grafted onto the same rootstock) trained in this way will enable you to fit up to three different varieties into this minute space. This will unfortunately confine you to growing different sorts of apples and pears as it is unlikely you will find family plum and cherry trees.

Remember, when planting any fruit tree, that the union between the grafted variety and the rootstock must not be buried or the dwarfing effect of the stock will be drastically reduced. (Pruning of trained fruit trees is dealt with on page 124.

STRAWBERRIES

Because you so often see strawberries cultivated in dedicated beds, it is not often realised that they actually make good ground cover. In my more traditional orchard, I grow them in the soil under the fruit trees and they yield perfectly satisfactorily (though not producing bumper crops or prize-winning berries) for many years before they have to be removed to give the ground a rest for a couple of years.

In this mini-orchard, they are used initially as an edging to the front of the bed. The runners that are produced can either be removed or pegged down in empty bits of soil to form ground cover in a similar way to my much larger fruit garden. Properly fed and watered, both the original plants and their offspring will fruit for several years. When cropping falls off to the point where they cease to be a viable proposition, they should be removed and the ground kept free from strawberries for a year or two. To ensure that it earns its keep, any empty soil can be planted up with mini-vegetables or annual herbs.

KEEPING THE MINI-ORCHARD HAPPY

As with all intensive cropping schemes, the soil very rapidly becomes exhausted unless it is regularly cared for. To maintain a good structure, mulch in autumn or spring with well-rotted farm-yard manure or good quality garden compost. You will also need to top-dress to keep the nutrient level high. Bone meal applied in autumn to the soil surface at 250g/sq m (8oz/sq yd) and lightly forked in, plus a spring dressing of either a slow-release balanced fertiliser according to the manufacturer's instructions or a com-pound organic feed such as fish, blood and bone added at 125g/sq m (4oz/sq yd) should do this. The well-being of all the plants will be helped by using a regular foliar feed according to instructions, throughout the growing season.

Always ensure that the soil is kept moist. This is particularly important during hot, dry weather and when the fruit is swelling. Regular water may be applied using perforated hose 'woven' through the bed. This may be attached to a timing device if desired.

Fruit at One's Elbow

CULTIVATING FRUIT IN THE HOME AND CONSERVATORY

If you have a sunny room with large windows or patio doors, or, better still, a conservatory with enough winter heat to take the chill off it, you can considerably extend your range of home-pro-duced fruit. In early summer, the container-grown plants may be moved onto the patio. When the temperature starts to fall in autumn, they should be moved inside again, preferably to a posi-tion that is as light as possible and not too warm, so that they can rest over winter.

HOUSEPLANT FRUIT

Certain fruiting plants can cope with a wide range of conditions and therefore are as happy in the living room as they are in the conservatory. Among these are the pomegranate, the **dwarf olive** and the **Canary Island banana**. These all require a light position with some direct sunlight at all times of the year and a comfortable domestic winter temperature, so they make good houseplants. They can be stood outdoors during the summer in a very sheltered, sunny spot, but are quite happy if they never experience the great outdoors beyond the French windows.

FRUIT FOR THE CONSERVATORY

Other ornamental fruiting plants are technically suitable for use as houseplants, but their size at maturity often makes this impractical, while others need more light, a lower average temperature and a more buoyant atmosphere than they are likely to experience in most homes.

Among these is the **edible passion fruit** which, although it can be treated as a houseplant, needs space to produce decent fruit. It can be kept 'room-sized' by training on a wire hoop and pruning heavily, but under these conditions it is unlikely to bear fruit of any quality and quantity. Trained on a trellis in a conservatory, however, and given enough space to wander freely, it will produce prodigious crops in a good season.

Passion fruit plants need a large tub and a soil-based compost, such as John Innes No 3, in which they will remain happily without replanting for several years, provided they are fed regularly throughout the growing season (a tomato feed is suitable). In early spring, the top few centimetres (about 2in) of compost may be renewed and replaced with fresh compost of the same kind.

To conserve moisture and improve the appearance of the pot, it may be topped off with a layer of pea shingle or ornamental chippings, but this must be removed before repotting or top dressing with fresh compost.

Pruning really consists of keeping the plants within bounds. The lighter the pruning, the more fruit will be produced, but after a year or two the plants will get very large and require drastic treatment. You will probably get as many passion fruit as you are likely to need if you cut the plant down to about 1m (3ft) above the level of the compost every year in early spring.

Indoor grapevines grow much too large for the home, but can be trained along the ridge and/or eaves of a larger conservatory to provide summer shade for other plants beneath.

Grapevines must have good ventilation throughout the growing season or the fruit and leaves will be affected by powdery mildew, a fungal disease that is easier to prevent (by good growing conditions) than it is to cure. Spraying with a fungicide suitable for edible crops helps to prevent the disease getting worse, but may not stop the fruit being damaged and is not practical in a furnished conservatory.

Tender grapevines are ideal subjects for conservatories that are used a lot in summer, then shut off with little or no heat during the rest of the year. All grapevines need to become dormant during winter and it is during this time that they should be pruned, shortening all side growths back to one bud on the main branches (rods).

Ideally, the root of the young grape vine should be planted outdoors and the top growth brought into the conservatory through a hole in the wall, but this is not always practical. Otherwise, it must be grown in a very large pot and should never be allowed to become short of either food or moisture or the crop will be severely affected. It should always be planted in a soil-based compost.

Citrus fruits (orange, lemon, lime, grapefruit, etc.,) are not happy with stuffy growing conditions and excessively high temperatures and they must have plenty of light to remain healthy. You will sometimes see them for sale as large houseplants, but they are unlikely to last long under such conditions and are much more at home in a cool (but not entirely unheated) conservatory during the winter, where they can enjoy a resting period, and outdoors on the patio in summer.

Citrus plants cannot tolerate high levels of alkalinity in the compost. If the soil is alkaline, their leaves eventually turn yellow (a condition known as lime-induced chlorosis) and, untreated, the bushes will eventually die. For this reason, they are often potted in a proprietary ericaceous compost, but this becomes 'played out' after one or two years, necessitating regular repotting.

The alternative is to mix John Innes No 3 compost half-and-half by volume with ericaceous compost. This makes the growing medium lighter and less acid while remaining substantial enough to support on-going growth for several seasons.

Specific citrus feeds are available, but they are expensive and most citrus plants supplied for home cultivation will flower and fruit just as readily if fed with tomato fertiliser. Preferably, they should be watered with soft water or rain water (not artificially softened) but, unless your tap water is very hard, it will be a long time before the plants begin to show signs of chlorosis, and this can be remedied if caught in time.

As soon as any leaves begin to lose their deep green colour, start feeding with an ericaceous plant food (sometimes called rhododendron fertiliser) according to the instructions on the packaging and continue to use this in addition to the regular feed unless or until you start using soft water.

Unless the conservatory is very cool in winter, most citrus will produce flowers, and therefore fruit, all the year round. If this is the case, feeding should continue year-round as well, although during the winter it should be less frequent – about half as often as in summer is adequate.

Citrus do not need regular pruning and most of those offered for conservatory growing are naturally compact varieties and so never outgrow their positions. If you do feel they are getting rather large for their surroundings, all varieties may be cut back by any amount during the growing season (mainly from April to August) and will soon produce new shoots.

INDOOR FRUIT FROM SEED

Tender fruiting plants raised from seeds, stones and pips, such as avocado pear, lemon, tangerine, lychee and mango may be treated in a similar way to conservatory citrus fruit. They all have their little idiosyncrasies, but in general will cope quite well with such conditions.

Unlike indoor fruit specially developed for home cultivation, the growth of seed-raised fruit may be erratic, untidy or over-large, depending on the type and variety of fruit involved. You are unlikely to get plants that are as attractive or useful as those from specialist nurserymen, but if you have the space, it can be interesting to have a go.

PEACHES, NECTARINES AND APRICOTS

Most indoor varieties of these fruits do not lend themselves to tub cultivation and are best grown as fans on the inside wall of the conservatory. Ideally, they should be grown in open soil or large, raised bed and, while some older, traditional conservatories may be able to provide these conditions, the construction of most modern types does not allow for this sort of thing. They also like a dormant period during winter, which is not possible if you want to use your conservatory all the year round.

However, if you are able to provide such conditions, try peach 'Royal George', nectarine 'Elruge' or apricot 'Isabella'. Pruning is the same as for members of the peach family grown outdoors.

FIGS

Tender figs are a better proposition for conservatory cultivation since, grown in pots, the normally over-strong growth is well curbed and the production of fruit continues undaunted. Generally, repotting should only be done when fruit production starts to fall.

MELONS

Melons are grown in containers in a similar way to cucumbers and courgettes but require higher temperatures and are therefore best cultivated under glass. Conservatory conditions are best, but in front of a sunny patio door can also be successful.

The easiest way to produce juicy melon fruits is to grow two plants in a good-quality growing bag. Make drainage holes in the base of the growing bag and stand it on a tray to avoid water running all over the floor. You will have to support the plants with canes or, preferably, a purpose-designed growing bag support that fastens the base of the canes to the underside of the growing bag for extra stability.

Melon plants may also be grown in individual, large pots. As the fruits swell, you will need to support them to prevent their breaking down the plants. You can do this by making cradles for them out of old tights, which can then be tied onto the main supporting canes. Plenty of water at all times is the secret to producing large, sweet, juicy melons.

NOTE

Growing deciduous fruit in a domestic conservatory has the major drawback of falling leaves in autumn. This can be very irritating if you are using the structure as another living room!

4

WHERE THERE'S MUCK THERE'S... SATISFACTION

Compost-making on the Patio

If your conception of compost is an untidy, dehydrated pile of branches and stalks at the bottom of the garden, or, worse still, a stinking, slimy mess of rotting grass clippings, you may be inclined to give this section a miss. However, it is possible to make something much more pleasant than this, which will give you the satisfaction of knowing that your garden and kitchen waste are not contributing to the increasing problem of domestic waste, while saving you money on peat and peat substitutes for potting compost additives and soil conditioners.

You may be horrified to learn that, whether you have a garden that can be measured in acres or one little more than a paved sitting area, the best place to make at least some of your compost is often, in fact, the patio, although if you have a lot of garden rubbish you may need to make more compost elsewhere.

The patio is usually warm, sunny and sheltered and placing your compost container within easy access of the back door will obviate the temptation to dispose of your kitchen waste in the dustbin as the quickest and easiest way of tidying up.

SUCCESSFUL PATIO COMPOSTING

THE CONTAINER

Always use a purpose-designed composter or bin. This will keep the rubbish tidy and help it to warm up quickly. Make sure you can access the contents at the base of the bin easily, preferably by means of a sliding side -wall or hatch. This will be the compost to use first and, if you remove it on a regular basis and keep adding to the top, you should eventually be able to provide yourself with a regular and constant supply of high quality compost.

The composter does not need a base but, if it is provided with one, it should contain drainage holes to allow excess liquid to drain away. Nor does it need ventilation holes. If the correct composting materials are used in the right combinations, there will be enough air entering the bin to allow aerobic decomposition. The more holes there are in a compost container, the more difficult it is for the contents to heat up sufficiently to make good quality compost.

A square bin will make more compost than a round one for the amount of space it occupies. Insulating the sides of the bin will speed up the composting process. Insulated plastic bins are now available, so it pays to seek one out. Otherwise use a wooden one, as wood has better insulating properties than thin plastic or metal. A wooden bin should be treated with a plant-friendly preservative before starting to use it.

Make sure that the bin has a lid. This will keep out rain and prevent insects and vermin being attracted by the contents. Waste vegetation will not compost successfully if it is too wet and it is easier to dampen the contents if necessary than to dry out a waterlogged bin.

Place the bin in a sunny position. Obviously, for the sake of the appearance of the patio, it is best to position it discreetly if possible, although if you choose a bin with a pleasing design, it will not be too intrusive, especially if you group attractive pots, troughs or similar containers around it.

It is often advised to place the bin direct on the earth so that worms and other creatures that work on vegetation to break it down can access the compost. In fact, this is not necessary and having a hard base such as concrete or paving slabs makes it much easier to shovel out the compost when it is ready. I find that worms will appear in a compost bin regardless of whether it stands on soil or paving, but perfectly satisfactory compost can be made without the presence of worms at all as the rapid breaking down of most vegetable waste is done mainly by aerobic bacteria.

THE RIGHT MATERIALS

Almost all fresh vegetable waste and some other kinds of waste, can be composted, provided it is of a suitable size. You are most likely to have some or all of the following:

1   Kitchen waste, including vegetable parings, fruit peel
    and citrus skins; tea-leaves and bags and coffee grounds
2   Shredded paper and cardboard
3   Shredded woody stems and sawdust
4   Pet and human hair
5   The contents of the vacuum cleaner
6   Autumn leaves
7   Prunings and trimmings
8   Grass clippings
9   Annual weeds
10 Discarded bedding plants
11 Vegetable plants at the end of their season (e.g. tomatoes,
    peppers, runner beans, etc)
12 Hedge clippings

Ideally, leaves should be rotted down separately from other vegetable waste, as they contain a large amount of lignin, which breaks down more slowly and so can slow up compost-making. However, provided that they are mixed well with softer waste, such as potato peelings, cabbage leaves, tea-leaves, grass clippings and the like, they will not slow the rotting process all that much.

Autumn leaves that are composted separately will eventually form what is known as 'leaf mould'. It is a very useful material as it is unlikely to contain weed seeds or significant amounts of pests and diseases and therefore makes a very good substitute for peat, particularly where an acid medium is required, for example, as a top dressing for a peat bed.

Leaf mould may be used straight from the heap as a soil conditioner or mulch. If you want to add it to potting compost, it is best to work it through a medium-gauge garden sieve or riddle first to make the texture finer. It should then look rather like sphagnum moss peat.

Whereas most garden waste is decomposed by bacteria, leaves from deciduous plants at the end of the growing season and other mainly woody substances, such as sawdust and shredded woody prunings, are mostly broken down by various forms of fungi.

There are a few items that are not suitable for adding to a healthy compost bin. These are mainly:

1   Pest and disease ridden plants. In theory, the decomposing material should heat up sufficiently to destroy pests and diseases, but on the assumption that it does not, it is better to exclude them completely.

2   Perennial weeds with roots. You will find it difficult to get your compost to heat up enough to destroy these completely. If you want to use your compost as a peat substitute in potting composts, it is better to exclude seeding annual weeds too since some seeds may still be viable, even in the best-made compost.

3   Cooked food, even of vegetable origin. This will smell bad as it rots and will also attract vermin and flies.

4   Pet waste (e.g. dog faeces and the contents of the cat's litter tray). Some pet waste is, however, acceptable, such as that from rabbit and other herbivore pet hutches and cages, and bird droppings in small quantities, which will actually speed up decomposition.

5   Meat and meat products, whether cooked or raw.

PRODUCING THE BEST COMPOST

Suitable waste materials may be composted at any time of the year but you will get usable compost much quicker when the weather is warm. However, rotting down will still continue in winter, so do carry on adding to your bin.

Never add too much of any one type of material, for example grass clippings or other wet or sappy rubbish, coarse, woody waste, autumn leaves or paper. To work efficiently, you should alternate shallow layers of coarse and fine matter. If you find you are getting too much coarse, dry rubbish in the bin, try adding some fresh lawn clippings. If you do not have a lawn or do not remove your clippings, you may find a neighbour only too happy to help you out!

Large pieces of rubbish, like branches, newspapers and sheets of cardboard should be cut or torn up small before composting. You may find a shredder useful here. Domestic shredders are not the noisy, inefficient, anti-social beasts they were a decade ago. The best are now virtually silent in operation and will cope with a whole day's work without constantly becoming blocked, providing the right materials are fed into them.

If you intend to put animal or human hair into your bin, spread it out extremely thinly and mix it in with plenty of vegetable matter. Compost, as it rots, should have a distinctive, but not unpleasant smell. It should certainly not be offensive to anyone sitting or standing in the vicinity of the compost bin. In any case, if the lid fits properly, any smell will be very faint. If the compost does smell disagreeable, it is not rotting properly. Bad smells are usually produced by anaerobic bacteria, which can function without air. They are an indication that your compost is much too wet or that you have added too much wet, soft garden waste, like grass clippings, all at once.

There is no need to add layers of soil between the waste, as you often see recommended – I find this slows up rotting and does not improve the texture at all. Nor is it necessary to 'turn' compost (mix it all up regularly and bring the bottom to the top), another recommendation of the 'old school' of garden compost devotees. This can also slow up decomposition by cooling the rotting materials down. However, it is sometimes useful to pull some of the previous layer up with a fork and mix it in with the most recently added waste. This helps to make the texture of the compost consistent.

Various compost accelerators are available. If you are making your compost properly, these should not be necessary, although some of them do help to produce it more quickly and some have ingredients claimed to 'improve' the quality of the finished product, making it less acid, for example.

If your compost looks rather dry and does not seem to be breaking down quickly enough, try adding a little warm water, but do not over-wet it.

WHEN AND HOW TO USE THE FINISHED PRODUCT

This varies according to the time of year but, in general, allow about six months before you inspect the compost at the base of the container.

The finished compost should be nearly black or very dark brown, moist but not wet, crumbly and smelling slightly 'earthy'. You should not be able to identify individual ingredients. If they still look like hedge trimmings or rose prunings, for example, you have put unsuitably large pieces in the bin, added too much of the same sort of material all at once, or not waited long enough.

Garden compost may be used in the garden in several ways. Straight from the bin, it can be dug into the ground and mixed with the soil in larger raised beds, to improve the texture and introduce air. It can also be spread on the top of the soil to control weeds and conserve soil moisture. To be most effective, the

NOTE
Garden compost is not a fertiliser, so it should not be used exclusively for feeding plants. It does contain nutrients and trace elements in small quantities, but the composition varies according to the type of waste that has been composted, and to be of any use as a plant food you would need several kilos (pounds) of it to do the same job as a few grams (ounces) of fertiliser, whether organic or inorganic in origin.

mulch should be 8–10cm (3–4in) deep. If you are absolutely sure that your compost does not contain any diseased plant material or weed seeds it may be sieved to break it up into a fine, peat-like material and used instead of peat or proprietary peat substitute in soil-based composts.

5

FUN FOR ALL THE FAMILY
Home-grown Produce for the Barbecue

In my last book, *The Kitchen Garden Yearbook*, I mentioned the brothers and sisters, Hayden, Rhia, Joshua and Jodie. For this book they demonstrate how to grow food fit for a feast.

I asked each of them to raise a crop in a container that we could eat by the end of the summer school holidays at a barbecue to be organised on their patio by their parents, Keith and Susan. They could, of course, pick anything before this time if it was ready, but the deadline for the end-of-project meal was the late August.They were warned that if at any time before this one or more of them lost interest, there would be no mention in the book. You will realise that as this section has been included, the children did, in fact, see their undertaking successfully through.

In May, they had four identical, rectangular wooden boxes made by the local sheltered workshop where Susan works. These were much cheaper, better constructed and more practical for what we were trying to achieve than they would have found at most garden centres. They were treated with a plant-friendly wood preservative and had drainage holes drilled in the base.

None of the children had grown anything seriously before. The two girls had started children's 'mini-greenhouse' kits of easy vegetables and annuals the previous summer and were quite enthusiastic for a short time but, as the summer wore on, other attractions took over and they lost interest. I did not therefore want to give them anything too ambitious for their first serious project, so I rejected the idea of growing anything too difficult from seed.

First, we had to decide what things we were most likely to want as an accompaniment to the barbecued meat. It was essential that all the crops did well, as I felt that it could put them off gardening for life if things went wrong. I also felt that they should look as attractive as possible, both to maintain the children's interest and be decorative container features in their own right as they were to occupy a prominent position just outside the conservatory.

Anything that could be used in a salad was the obvious choice, but they should all be pick-and-come-again varieties so they could take over the containers for the whole of the season without replanting.

We started with 'Red and Green Salad Bowl' lettuce, which was allocated by default to Hayden's box as he was away playing football at the time, so the other three had the pick of the crops when the big planting up took place at the beginning of June.

I had purposely left planting until late in the season as the crops would be grown entirely outside and I could be quite sure there would be no disasters through late cold snaps.

As this was a project that could be copied by the children's friends, any half-hardy plants should be easy to obtain, so we opted for the garden centre of the local branch of a big DIY outlet. To go with lettuce, we needed tomatoes and managed to find three very good plants of 'Alicante', although this was not my first choice since it is an old variety and there are better ones around for outside container cultivation. Jodie thought she would have a go with these.

Peppers were the obvious choice as a third salad vegetable but, by this time of year, there were no decent plants left, so we decided to have a stab at aubergines instead, as there was still

Hayden making drills for lettuce seed

no shortage of good plants of these. Every part of the plant – leaves, flowers and fruit – is extremely attractive and therefore appealing as a patio plant, but I have always considered aubergines rather a tricky crop since they need a long growing season and are reputed to do best under glass. However, Rhia said that she was prepared to have a try. Rhia is definitely the one with the natural flair for gardening, particularly herb growing, so I knew she would work hard to get good results. The problem was that, unlike peppers, you cannot just slice up aubergines and add them to a salad or stick them on skewers and barbecue them, but I felt we could sort out the problem of how we could integrate them into the meal when the time came.

Carl the greyhound

We needed something sweet to finish with, so I obtained twelve plug plants of 'Temptation' strawberries from Mr. Fothergill's Seeds. These appealed to Joshua, so everyone was satisfied with his or her own lot.

Finally, partly to brighten up the project but also as a natural control for whitefly and aphids, we bought six French marigold plants, three for the tomato box and three for the aubergines. The boxes were filled with soil-less compost from another DIY outlet (because it was the most inexpensive that we could find and we were working to a budget) and I then showed each child in

Rhia planting aubergines

Rhia's box of aubergines and French marigolds

turn how to sow or plant the crop in question. The boxes were then placed (with some adult help!) in a sunny, south-west facing spot on the patio and the children – and mum and dad, who are not really gardeners – were shown how to water correctly, checking frequently by poking a finger into the compost to see if it was dry and, if so, applying water until it ran out at the base.

I recommended that, to simplify feeding and because all the plants, with the exception of the newly sown lettuce, were quite well-grown, they gave all the boxes a weekly watering with Maxicrop Tomato Fertiliser. Last, they were warned what would happen if they didn't look after them!

In fact, they were most diligent, and the results were splendid. Jodie's hard work resulted in huge crops of tomatoes, without a whitefly in sight or a vestige of blossom end rot although, because the weather during the second half of summer was not very good, most of the fruits ripened late, long after the children had returned to school.

Rhia grew some nice, big, shiny aubergines, despite an early setback when slugs chewed large holes in the leaves. Josh couldn't resist sampling each 'Temptation' strawberry as it ripened, which was quite amazing, as up to then he hadn't liked fresh fruit of any sort. And Hayden couldn't keep up with his lettuce, even though he picked leaves every day and gave much away.

The barbecue was a great success. Even Carl the greyhound tucked in with relish. Rhia and her young friend Hannah, who had come for the day, spent much time making a big bowl of salad out of the lettuce and tomatoes, garnishing it well with any of Rhia's

Joshua with 'Temptation'

Hayden with a glut of lettuce

herbs we felt would be suitable. We made a bowl of fruit salad with Josh's strawberries. As for the aubergines … Sue and I eventually came up with the idea of slicing them and frying them with the onions for the burgers and sausages and they proved to be quite delicious.

The project has certainly fired the enthusiasm of both the children and their parents and it is to be hoped that it will now become an annual venture. There are many vegetables and some good soft fruits that can be grown in this way with little gardening knowledge and only basic equipment. If a cold greenhouse or conservatory is available for the raising of half-hardy vegetables from seed, the choice is even wider.

Preparing the barbecue vegetables

SOME GOOD, 'FAMILY-ORIENTATED' VEGETABLES FOR PATIO CULTIVATION

FOR DIRECT SOWING INTO CONTAINERS

SALAD LEAVES:
Leaf lettuce
Chicory
Rocket
Spinach 'Samish F1'
Lamb's lettuce
American land cress

ROOT VEGETABLES:
Round-rooted or 'finger' carrots
Mini-beetroot such as 'Pronto': pick early leaves
sparingly and use as spinach substitute, then allow
roots to develop
Turnip 'Tokyo Cross F1': pick early leaves sparingly and
cook as 'spring greens', then allow roots to develop
Radishes
Early potatoes

LEAF VEGETABLES:
Chard
Perpetual spinach
Dwarf beans

HALF-HARDY VEGETABLES:
Tomatoes
Cucumbers
Courgettes and squashes
Peppers
Aubergines (early varieties only)
Cape gooseberries
Tomatillos

FRUIT:
Strawberries – particularly perpetual fruiting types
Blueberries
Cranberries

TAKE IT EASY: AUTOMATIC WATERING AND FEEDING

The main drawback to growing anything – edible or ornamental – in containers is the fact that, unlike plants grown in the open ground, they dry out rapidly and therefore need constant attention to watering. Because nutrients are quickly washed out of the compost if sufficient water is given and because the plants are grown in a restricted space, they also require more regular and careful feeding than they would in an unfettered situation.

Unless you are a dedicated gardener with few interests in life other than heaving heavy watering cans up and down the patio for a large part of the day, some mechanisation is essential to make growing vegetables and fruit in containers a serious proposition.

Fortunately, in recent years many automatic watering devices have come onto the market for the home gardener, and this has revolutionised our approach to gardening in general and cultivation in containers in particular. By using the right installation, the effort of regular and frequent watering and feeding can be taken off your hands completely, leaving you free to get on with other things or even go away on holiday for weeks on end without having to rely on good-natured neighbours, while your containers continue to burgeon with good health.

Over the last decade, I have experimented with many devices offered by different manufacturers, and have found the most successful of the off-the-peg micro-irrigation watering schemes for the amateur gardener to be that offered by Hozelock. This is widely available from garden centres and similar outlets, is simple to tailor to one's own requirements and easy to install.

This type of automatic irrigation is based on a 13mm (0.5in) black plastic supply tube laid around the garden where automatic watering is required. This is connected to an outside tap by means of a pressure regulator to convert the mains water pressure to 1.5 bar so that the system works correctly.

The tube can be buried in the ground, covered with mulch or hidden among the greenery. In my own case, where it is not possible to do this, it has been attached discreetly to the base of the wall with pipe clips, just above the surface of the patio paving.

The water is taken to the plants, tubs, hanging baskets and the like by means of 4mm (0.16in) black plastic micro-tube, fitted into the supply tube by means of special connectors. This can

be tacked onto a wall or fence if necessary for neatness with micro-tube fencing clips or cable clips.

The water is applied directly to the surface of the compost or soil when it is wanted via fixed rate or, preferably, adjustable drippers. These can be finely adjusted to apply anything from a very slow drip to a serious sprinkle, depending on need.

The micro-bore tube can be pegged to the compost just below the dripper. This prevents the tube becoming dislodged resulting in the water missing the container and ensures that the water goes to exactly the right spot – that is, the base of the plant, just above the surface of the compost.

The system, at its most basic, is operated by turning the outside tap on and off. This does away with the necessity for carrying heavy cans of water around, but you are still tied to the home at least one period during the day, while you operate the tap and check that the right amount of water is being given.

For complete freedom, you can add some kind of timer. There are many available today, from simple devices that dispense a given volume of water to sophisticated electronic controls that can be programmed to turn the water on and off several times a day and can be set so that they only operate on certain days of the week, which is useful early and late in the season. You will soon get to know if your plants are receiving too much or too little water and can then adjust the timer accordingly if necessary.

This will take care of watering for you, but to eliminate the tedium of this sort of manual regular maintenance altogether, you will also need some form of automated liquid fertiliser dispenser if you are not to be tied to a once- or twice-weekly feeding regime.

Curiously, the development of this type of automation has not kept pace over the years with micro-irrigation. At the date this book is written, there is only one in-line automatic feeding device (as opposed to hose-end feeders, of which there are many around, but

NOTE

It is a legal requirement that all outside taps that run off the mains water supply are fitted with a double check-valve to prevent any likelihood of dirty water getting back into the domestic water supply. Modern outside taps often incorporate such a valve, but if yours does not, non-return valves that can be screwed and locked onto the threaded end of the tap are widely available from plumbers' merchants, hardware shops, garden centres and DIY outlets.

all needing to be manually operated) widely available to the amateur gardener, although there are many on the commercial market.

This is the Phostrogen Thru'Hose Feeder, which is installed in-line after the pressure-reducing valve and is designed to dispense a measured amount of soluble fertiliser each time water passes through it. At present, it is only recommended for use with Phostrogen plant foods because of the specific dilution rates. This means that you can't use a different fertiliser, although the feeder can be adjusted to dispense variable concentrations of plant food depending on whether water passes through it more or less frequently (the more frequent the watering, the less food will be included).

Using this gadget, routine maintenance of plants in containers is reduced (theoretically) to merely checking the bowl periodically to make sure there is still fertiliser powder and topping it up if it has all been used. However, speaking from over a decade's experience of using automatic watering devices, if you do decide to become automated, it is prudent to keep a watchful eye on the system in general.

Drippers can become blocked with limescale and minute, undissolved particles of fertiliser. If you do not check them regularly, the first indication that you have a problem is when the plants in a particular container collapse through lack of water, placing them under the sort of strain which, if you are growing them as crops, they just do not need.

Connectors, elbows and the like may become detached so most of the water destined for your baskets and tubs is gushing out long before it reaches them.

Timers can (and do) go wrong: ironically, they always seem to go wrong in the 'off' position so that your plants receive no water at all, which is much worse than their being over-watered for a short period. Because nothing in life is ever foolproof, it is always wise to get a friend to check any automatically watered plants if you are away from home for more than a day or two. This said, few horticultural inventions of the last couple of decades have taken more routine drudgery out of gardening than automated watering and feeding and for the busy patio gardener it really is a 'must'.

APPENDIX 1
Recommended vegetable varieties for the patio gardener

AUBERGINES

These require a very warm situation outdoors and must be an early-ripening variety for success. Alternatively, they make neat, attractive conservatory plants.
'Black Beauty': nearly black, pear-shaped fruits that mature very early.
'Moneymaker F1': ripens well in the British climate.

BEANS

BROAD BEANS
'Lingo': a 'baby bean' with a short, stocky habit, producing a massive crop of sweet, pea-sized beans.
'Sutton Large': crops of normal-sized beans on compact, sturdy plants.

DWARF FRENCH BEANS
'Ferrari Slim': handsome beans of a healthy, dark green shade.
'Purple Queen': glossy, round, purple beans. Can be mixed with 'Safran' to good effect.
'Purple Teepee': produces a profusion of purple beans borne above the foliage and so make attractive ornamental plants.
'Safran': pencil-thin, bright yellow pods with great ornamental value.

DWARF RUNNER BEANS
'Flamenco': a new mixture of 'Hammond's Dwarf Scarlet', 'Hestia' and 'Snow White', as useful for its floral display as for its great selection of high-yielding runner beans.
'Hestia': a dwarf 'Painted Lady' with abundant red and white flowers and long, straight, stringless pods.

RUNNER BEANS
'Kelvedon Stringless': early ripening, this variety responds well to pinching out where space is limited.
'Painted Lady': an old variety, great for patio cultivation because of its compact habit, comparatively short beans and abundance of red and white flowers.

BRASSICAS

CABBAGE
'Cape Verde F1': pointed summer Savoy/salad cross, can be eaten raw, used in stir-fries or cooked in the normal way.
'Greyhound Compact': pointed hearts. A favourite with gardeners for many years.
'Minicole F1': hard, tight, little heads stand for months over the summer.
'Rodima F1': compact red cabbage with tight heads. If the main cabbage is cut just before maturity, the stalk will produce several smaller heads later in the season.

'Sparkel F1': tender young leaves are eaten as 'spring greens'.

CALABRESE, CAULIFLOWER AND BROCCOLI

'Candid Charm F1' (cauliflower): produces delicious, tennis ball-sized heads for eating raw or cooked in July and August.
'Italian Sprouting' (broccoli): two or three container-grown plants will produce a succession of tasty spears in late winter and spring.
'Limelight F1' (cauliflower): pretty lime-green heads can be planted effectively amongst ornamentals.
'Red Lion' (cauliflower): rich purple heads make a practical alternative to ornamental kale in early winter bedding schemes.
'Romanesco Natalino' (calabrese): attractive, lime-green pinnacle heads of superb flavour.

KALE

'Redbor F1': tall variety with red-frilled leaves for summer or winter use. The colour is more pronounced in colder weather.
'Starbor F1': tender, dark green, curled leaves on compact plants.

KOHL RABI

'Kongo F1': fast-maturing brassica with a swollen root base at soil level. 'Kongo' is picked when golf ball-sized and grated raw in salads or boiled for around 20 minutes

until still crisp but tender.

CAPSICUMS (PEPPERS)

SWEET PEPPERS
'Redskin F1': suitable for growing outdoors on a warm, sunny patio. Heavy crop of boxy, slightly pointed fruits turn red when ripe.

CAYENNE PEPPER
Hot! Slim, pointed fruit can be dried or frozen when either green or red. Caution: don't touch sensitive parts of the body such as lips or eyes when handling the ripe fruit as it can cause severe irritation and burning.

CUCUMBERS, COURGETTES

COURGETTES
'Ambassador F1': Dark fruits are a perfect accompaniment to 'Sunburst'.
'Black Forest F1': a climbing variety which can be trained up a trellis. Near-black fruits retain their size over a long period and do not turn into marrows.
'Sunburst F1' (summer squash): tempting, butter-yellow fruits of a most unusual shape.

CUCUMBERS
'Bush Champion': a compact plant producing masses of

20cm (8in) fruits.
'Marketmore': a variety particularly suited to container cultivation, with manageable, straight fruit best picked at around 15–20cm (6–8in) long.
'Patiopik': low-growing, bush variety producing small, chubby cucumbers.

GARLIC

'Fleur de lys': easy variety for spring planting in the British climate.
'Mersley White': British-bred garlic for autumn planting that is capable of withstanding the UK winter.

HERBACEOUS PERENNIAL VEGETABLES

ASPARAGUS
A useful vegetable for flower arrangers, as the ferny foliage can be cut in moderation from mature plants.
'Connover's Colossal': the most popular and widely offered variety, producing early, thick stalks.
All-male plants: these are

preferable as all energy is channelled into producing non-seeding stalks. Many F1 varieties are now available, among the best being 'Franklim', 'Cito', 'Lucullus', 'Limbras' and 'Venlim'. They are invariably sold as crowns (young, bare-root plants) and cannot be raised from seed. Some companies are now offering module-raised plants, which are easy and quick to establish and are therefore ideal for incorporating into mixed borders. Look out for module-raised varieties like 'Jersey Giant' and 'Gijnlim' or, for something different, the deep purple-stemmed variety 'Purple Passion'.

GLOBE ARTICHOKE

A highly architectural, thistle-like plant with grey-green leaves and ball-shaped flower buds on sturdy stems about 1.2m (4ft) high. These buds are eaten before maturing into striking, huge, purple heads that are, however, useful for larger flower arrangements.

CARDOON

A similar plant of the same family producing smaller heads on taller stems. It is these stems that are cut into pieces and boiled until tender. Both cardoons and globe artichokes are excellent plants for the mixed or herbaceous border.

JERUSALEM ARTICHOKE

A perennial relative of the sunflower which grows 1.8–2.4m (6–8ft) tall during the summer and therefore makes a quick, functional screen. The knobbly tubers are dug up during the dormant period between November and March. They can be cooked like potatoes or made into soup and have a distinctive, smoky flavour. Chinese artichokes are cultivated and cooked in the same way.

GOOD KING HENRY

Also known as Lincolnshire spinach or mercury, this vegetable needs to be kept under control once established as it can become a nuisance and should never be allowed to seed. It can be used as a substitute for spinach and, although not spectacular in appearance, may be used as a foil for more striking plants around the patio.

SORREL

This can be used like spinach or good King Henry. The leaves are neater and more attractive than the latter and it can be used as a foliage edging around a rose bed or similar feature.

LEAF VEGETABLES

CHARD (SEAKALE BEET) AND SPINACH

'Bright Lights': a recently introduced variety with red, pink, purple, orange, red and white stems and midribs and green and bronze leaves.

Perpetual spinach: a high-yielding relative of beetroot, cooked and cultivated like spinach but much easier to grow, with a growing season of around twelve months if picked regularly.

Rhubarb chard: a highly decorative vegetable similar in form and function to Swiss chard, but with a dark, reddish-green outer leaf and a slightly thinner, bright red midrib.

Swiss chard: a vegetable with an outer leaf reminiscent of, and cooked like, spinach and a striking, thick white midrib that can be cooked like asparagus.

ONIONS AND SHALLOTS

BULBING ONIONS FROM SEED

'Paris Silverskin': produces tight, round bulbs for pickling.
'Vera Prima': early maturing variety which is suitable for harvesting young for pickling or allowed to mature further for use in cooking.

SPRING (BUNCHING) ONIONS

'Laser': crisp and mild
'North Holland Blood Red',
'Redmate' ('Little Wonder'): Attractive red skin that deepens in colour as the plants mature.
'White Lisbon Winter Hardy': similar to the above, but can be sown in late summer for winter and spring use.
'White Lisbon': still the most popular variety for salads, easy and prolific.

ONIONS FROM SETS

'British Bulldog': British-produced onion set with gold-skinned, good-sized bulbs.
'Centurion': yellow-skinned, semi-round bulbs. Good flavour and heavy crops.
'Orion A': 'Sturon' type onion with better storing potential and larger mature bulbs.
'Red Epicure: gourmet onion with deep red, shiny skin and crisp, white flesh.

SHALLOTS

'Santé': reddish-skinned variety that should be planted late and is therefore ideal for use among ornamental plants.

PEAS

EARLY

'Daybreak': probably the earliest pea with a heavy yield, good flavour and short, manageable haulms (stems).
'Douce Provence': very sweet, dwarf pea that does exceptionally well when autumn-sown.

SECOND EARLY/ MAIN CROP

'Hurst Green Shaft': slightly taller, but still, in my opinion, the best pea for all-round use. Pods can contain as many as 11 peas of an unsurpassable flavour.
'Little Marvel': an old favourite, dwarf and high-yielding.

MANGE TOUT AND SUGAR SNAP VARIETIES

'Dwarf Sweet Green': a well-flavoured, heavy producing mange tout pea.
'Sugar Bon': a dwarf version of sugar snap that produces hundreds of super-sweet, almost stringless pods.

ROOT VEGETABLES

BEETROOT

'Albina Vereduna': a white beetroot with attractive, wavy, green leaves that cook well as a spinach substitute when young.
'Modella': round, ruby red beets and attractive foliage.
'Pronto': best harvested at Ping-Pong ball size. Cook by steaming lightly to retain texture colour and sweetness.
Ornamental beet
'MacGregor's Favourite': a multi-purpose plant with attractive flowers, ornamental edible leaves and roots that are used in the same way as beetroot.

CARROTS

'Amini': classic carrot shape for harvesting as 'finger carrots'.
'Amsterdam Forcing 3 – Minicor': produces high quality baby carrots, equally delicious raw or cooked.
'Flyaway F1': a well-flavoured, medium-sized carrot with

special resistance to carrot fly.
'Mokum': fast-maturing, cylindrical carrot.
'Newmarket F1': recommended variety for pulling as 'finger carrots'.
'Pariska': cherry-sized carrots needing no preparation before use other than a good wash.
'Parmex': round roots ideal for pot and growing bag cultivation.

PARSNIPS

'Arrow': narrow-shouldered variety producing slim but substantial roots where space is limited.

POTATOES

As most patio-cultivated potatoes will be grown in pots and barrels, the choice of variety will largely depend on the accessibility of very small quantities of seed potatoes as it is not economical to buy a pre-packed kilo or more of top-price, top quality seed. For this reason, you may find it most convenient and economical to save a few tubers from a shop-bought bag of eating potatoes, especially if your main priority is to produce some potatoes of your own, however small the quantity.

An alternative is to buy small packs of young plants of micro-propagated rare varieties from specialist seed companies. Although expensive, this way of obtaining potato stock does give you an opportunity to experiment with uncommon varieties, many of which are strikingly coloured or oddly shaped – a good talking point if you enjoy entertaining and impressing your guests!

If you have some control over choice of varieties, personal preference regarding colour, texture and flavour will have the casting vote, so it is difficult to make recommendations. The following list is therefore a selection of varieties that have worked well for me when grown in containers.

First earlies

'Karlina': possibly the earliest potato to produce large quantities of good quality tubers for baking and chipping.
'Rocket': nearly as early as Swift, Rocket has waxy flesh and egg-shaped tubers
'Swift': a very early, white skinned, high-yielding all-rounder.
'Vanessa': attractive potatoes with yellow flesh and red skins. Not the earliest, but certainly one of the best.

Second earlies

'Alex': a new salad potato with a pleasing, creamy, waxy flesh and mild flavour.

'Nadine', 'Wilja' and 'Estima': three potatoes of recent years that are ideal for flavour, yield and reliability.

Maincrop

'Desirée': an extremely popular potato with a high yield, smooth red skin, excellent flavour and compact habit.
'King Edward': still the first choice for those who grow their own potatoes. Not the heaviest cropper, but unsurpassed for flavour, appearance and texture.
'Pink Fir Apple': this is my favourite 'novelty' potato, with its curious, elongated, knobbly tubers, pink skin and waxy flesh. Usually recommended as a salad potato, served cold, it is just as good when hot, retaining its new potato flavour even after it has been stored for several months.

RADISH

For the greatest variety, choose a mixed packet of radish seed. Most seed companies offer mixtures, the most popular varieties for inclusion generally being 'Cherry Belle', 'French Breakfast', 'Long White Icicle', 'Pink Beauty' and 'Sparkler'.

TURNIP

'Market Express': similar to 'Tokyo Cross' and best harvested when golf-ball sized.

'Tokyo Cross F1': a fast-maturing turnip that is sown late and best pulled when small, although even large ones retain their flavour and texture.

SALADS

LETTUCE
'Bijou': handsome, glossy red leaves, ideal for impact in a mixed salad.

'Cut-and-come-again' types
'Lollo Biondo': pale green version of 'Lollo Rosso'.
'Lollo Rosso': frilled green leaves tipped with red.
'Red and Green Salad Bowl Mixed': a mixture of red and bright green 'oak-leaved' lettuce types. Can be picked a few leaves at a time over a long period.
'Spiky': produces attractive, heavily serrated leaves. Compact habit suitable for close planting.

Butterhead/cabbage types
'Dynamite': compact heads with bright green leaves and a tight heart.
'Kendo': similar habit flavour to 'Little Gem' with red-tinged outer leaves.
'Tom Thumb': an old favourite, easy to grow and quick to mature.

Cos lettuce
'Little Gem': solid hearts and sweet flavour make this still a favourite with grower and chef alike.
'Pinokkio': dwarf Cos with a fairly open habit and dark, shiny, crisp leaves of crisp texture.

Miniature crisp/iceberg types
'Crispino': small, light green hearts. Can be harvested mature or picked a few leaves at a time.
'Mini Green': tennis-ball-sized, ideal for one meal.

OTHER SALAD LEAF VEGETABLES
Chicory (endive): Adds a tangy, piquant flavour to leaf and mixed salads.
'Frisee Frisela': forms a dense heart or can be picked young, a few leaves at a time.
'Pain de Sucre': Cos lettuce-type hearts need no blanching.

'Très Fine Maraîchère Coquette': Attractive, bright green, curled leaves.
Lamb's lettuce (corn salad) Smooth, shiny green leaves add a distinctive flavour to salads.
American (land) cress: An easily grown alternative to watercress with a similar peppery flavour.
Rocket: A quick maturing salad plant with spicy, pungent leaves, now popular as an essential ingredient of leaf salads.
Salad burnet: An ornamental, perennial herb with a faintly bitter, nutty flavour reminiscent of cucumber.
Spinach 'Samish F1': A dual purpose, compact variety with dark green, Savoy cabbage-textured leaves that can be picked young and eaten raw in salads or allowed to grow larger for use as a cooked, green vegetable.

'WINDOWSILL' SALAD PLANTS

Alfalfa: sprouted in a similar way to fenugreek, alfalfa imparts a mild, green pea flavour when used as a garnish.
Brassica seeds (cabbage, cauliflower, Brussels sprout, kale, broccoli, etc): these can be sprouted like mustard and cress or alfalfa and eaten when at about the same

stage as cress. It is a good way of using up surplus brassica seeds. Radish and turnip are particularly tasty treated in this way. Try also beetroot, spring onions and carrots.

Chinese bean sprouts (Mung beans): can be grown in the same way as mustard and cress, but forced in the dark in a warm place, such as the airing cupboard. Alternatively, they may be sprouted in large glass jars on the windowsill, but the sprouts will be greener, shorter and less tender.

Cress 'Fine Curled': can be grown on wet blotting paper, damp kitchen paper or moist cotton wool or in small containers of peat-based compost.

Fenugreek: best sprouted green using the glass jar technique (see page 63). Harvest when just over 1cm (0.5in) long for strongest curry flavour; older shoots are still tasty but milder.

Mustard White: grown in the same way as cress. To crop at the same time as cress, sow four days later.

Salad cress 'Polycress': a blend of mustard and a new variety of cress seeds that mature at the same time, avoiding the necessity for staggered sowings.

SQUASHES (PUMPKINS)

'Baby Bear': comparatively small fruits with thick skins and succulent flesh. Popular with children.
'Baby Boo': white or yellow miniature pumpkin with light, mealy flesh that tastes rather like chestnuts. Can be baked like potatoes.

WINTER SQUASH
These mature from August until the frosts and can then be stored in a cool place for use over the winter. The fruits are often ornamental and highly attractive.
'Becky Heavy': grapefruit-sized fruit, good for baking.
'Cream of the Crop': yellow skin and mild flavour.
'Onion Squash': yellow fruits with same shape and texture externally as an very large onion. Sweet, nutty flavour.
'Rolet': high-yielding, with green fruits turning yellow when mature and aromatic, apricot-coloured flesh.
'Table Ace': heart-shaped, blackish-green fruits with peach-coloured flesh of a distinctive flavour.

SWEET CORN

'Ambrosia F1': extra sweet, two-coloured cobs.
'Champ': early-maturing, large cobs. Grows well anywhere.

'Maïs Multicolores': a decorative sweet corn with yellow, dark red, white and nearly black grains. Can be steamed or grilled.

'Minipop': a 'baby corn' that is eaten whole when young, either raw or lightly steamed.
'Strawberry Popcorn': novelty maize with little red cobs that can be cooked in the normal way or made into popcorn.

TOMATOES

'Brasero': has a spreading, bushy habit ideal for pots and containers, and bright red, very sweet fruit.
'Dombello F1': a 'beefsteak' tomato with huge fruits. Requires a warm, sunny position if grown outdoors.
'Nectar F1': an attractive variety for the conservatory or by the patio door, providing 'vine-ripened' cherry tomatoes that will last on the plant for around two weeks, ensuring a superb taste. 'Aranca F1' is similar.

'Precious F1': the variety for cooking and preserving. Plum-shaped with few seeds and thin skins.

'Shirley F1': classic tomato with excellent resistance to most tomato problems.

'Sugar Pearl F1': long trusses of sweet, cherry tomatoes.

'Sun Baby': a cherry-sized yellow tomato with a tangy yet sweet flavour.

'Sunset F1': a really sweet, orange cherry tomato yielding over 30 fruits per pound.

'Tigerella': bright red fruits with orange stripes make this variety popular for patio decoration.

'Tumbler F1': the variety for hanging baskets, with a dwarf, spreading habit and masses of ornamental, well-flavoured, cherry-sized tomatoes.

UNUSUAL HALF-HARDY VEGETABLES

The seedlings of these vegetables are generally raised indoors in the same way as tomatoes, peppers, cucumbers and the like. The young plants are then planted out in pots, growing bags and similar containers when they are large enough and are placed on a warm, sheltered patio or in a well-ventilated conservatory for cropping.

CAPE GOOSEBERRY
(Physalis peruviana)
A relative of the ornamental Chinese lantern, which it closely resembles, the Cape gooseberry is becoming popular with the more adventurous cook. The sour, orange fruits have slight gooseberry flavour and can be used in salads, jam, fruit salads and the like.

An ornamental, climbing vegetable for a sunny trellis, with decorative leaves and scented flowers, followed by fruits resembling misshapen miniature cucumbers. The unripe fruits are picked when about the size of an olive and can be added to salads or pickled in spiced vinegar.

KORILA
(Cyclanthera pedata)

(JAMBERRY) AND VIOLET TOMATILLO
(Physalis ixocarpa vars.)

Morelle de Balbis *(Solanum sisymbrifolium)*
The 1m (39in) prickly plants produce pretty, light blue flowers followed by red fruits surrounded by prickly shells. These have a sweet and sour flavour and can be used in a similar way to the related tomato.

TOMATILLOS
although resembling tomatoes when harvested, are also relatives of the Chinese lantern and Cape gooseberry and the fruits are produced inside an ornamental, lantern-like skin similarly. Tomatillos are much larger than cape gooseberries and are used in the same way as tomatoes, or can be made into an interesting and piquant jam.

UNUSUAL HARDY VEGETABLES

DRAGONHEAD
(Dracocephalum modavica)
An ornamental perennial plant that is usually raised from seed. The leaves are aniseed-flavoured and can be used in salads, soups, sauces and certain meat dishes. When established, it produces pretty, mauve-purple flowers during summer.

ORACHE
Red, green and white *(Atriplex hortensis vars.)*
This is cultivated like spinach, but can grow to over 2m (6ft) in height, with attractively decorative leaves that are a useful addition to a mixed border.

PARA CRESS, RED AND YELLOW
(Spilanthes fusca and S.oleracea)
These are sown in small pots around mid-May and transplanted into individual modules when large enough to handle. The seedlings are planted out in their final positions at the end of June. They will eventually produce orange-red or yellow flowers according to variety. The leaves are used sparingly in salads and as an alternative to basil. The red form has a bite to it; the yellow variety is milder.

STRAWBERRY SPINACH
A novelty vegetable-cum-fruit, related to the weed (or wild-flower, if you prefer!) fat hen. The leaves are cooked like spinach or used in leaf salads. After flowering, strawberry-like fruits with a bland, rather sweet flavour are produced that look pretty when used to decorate salads and savoury dishes; they can also be added to fruit salads where their insignificant flavour can be masked by more tasty ingredients.

APPENDIX 2
Herbs for confined spaces

ARCHITECTURAL CULINARY HERBS FOR INDIVIDUAL POT CULTIVATION, SCREENING OR HEDGING/EDGING

ANGELICA
(Angelica archangelica)
Short-lived herbaceous perennial. Its life may be prolonged by removing flower buds, but dried heads are useful for flower arranging. Height to 1.8m (6ft). Leaves and stalks can be cooked with tart fruits to reduce acidity. Stems may be candied for use in food decoration.

BAY *(Laurus nobilis)*
Evergreen shrub that may be trained and clipped to a variety of heights and shapes. Laurel-like leaves are used for flavouring a wide variety of savoury and sweet dishes.

CARAWAY *(Carum carvi)*
Biennial growing to 60cm (2ft) in height. Leaves in first season used for parsley-like flavouring in salads. Dried seeds at end of second year give characteristic flavouring to cakes, soups, coleslaw, etc. Roots resemble carrots and may be cooked like parsnips.

CHERVIL
(Anthriscus cerefolium)
An annual relative of cow parsley growing to around 50cm (20 in) with feathery leaves and white flowers. Leaves added to soups, fish and egg dishes just before serving, or used to garnish salads.

CORIANDER
(Coriandrum sativum)
Annual parsley relative growing to 90cm (3ft) when in

flower. Fresh leaves and seeds used widely in Indian, Egyptian, Peruvian and Greek cookery. Can be used to flavour confectionery, milk puddings and many meat and vegetable dishes. Cilantro is similar, but with larger, more decorative leaves.

COSTMARY OR ALECOST
(Balsamita major)
A herbaceous perennial with a creeping rootstock rather like that of tarragon and tall, leafy, branched stems up to 150cm (5ft) tall topped with daisy or button-like flowers. The leaves taste of lemon-mint and, since the plant does not die down in winter, it can be used as a mint or lemon balm substitute.

CUMIN *(Cuminum cyminum)*
Another annual relative of cow parsley of a similar height and habit to chervil. Ripe seeds are used in Indian, eastern European and Mexican cookery.

DILL *(Anethum graveolens)*
Yet another aromatic annual of the cow parsley family, with a distinctive, slightly aniseed flavour. Resembles fennel in habit (see below) but only grows to 60–100cm (24–40in). Leaves and seeds are used in many fish, meat and vegetable dishes.

FENNEL
(Foeniculum vulgare)
Herbaceous perennial of the same family as angelica, chervil, cumin, dill, etc. Height up to 1.5m (5ft) with feathery, green or bronze-tinted foliage according to variety and modestly attractive yellow, umbrella-like flower heads. Strong aniseed flavour. Chopped leaves and seeds are used with fish, salads, vegetables and soups.

HYSSOP *(Hyssopus officinalis)*
Aromatic, semi-evergreen, shrubby perennial reaching 60cm (24in) in height, with light blue, purplish-white, white or pink flowers. Strong, sagey-minty flavour. Leaves are used in salads, strongly flavoured soups, stews and meat dishes. Edible flowers may be used as salad garnish.

KOREAN MINT
(Agastache)
Aromatic, herbaceous perennials reaching a height of 60–120cm (24–48in), with mauve-purple flowers from June to September. Anise hyssop (Agastache anethiodora) has anise-scented leaves and can be used for an interesting flavour in salads. Korean mint (A. rugosa) has mint-scented foliage and can be used as a mint substitute. The leaves can be dipped in melted chocolate for a 'different' sweetmeat. Both species are

highly attractive to bees.

LAVENDER *(Lavandula sp.)*
Although lavender is mainly thought of as an aromatic herb, the edible flowers make an attractive garnish and the seeds give an interesting flavour to scones, cakes and some sweet dishes.

LEMON VERBENA
(Lippia citriodora)
Deciduous herb which will make 3m (10ft) if grown in a sunny, sheltered place in the open ground, but can be pruned to any size. The leaves have a very strong lemon flavour and can be added sparingly to salads, or may be mixed with mint to make a refreshing tea.

LOVAGE
(Levisticum officinalis)
Tall, herbaceous perennial relative of fennel, but with strong celery flavour. The young, finely chopped leaves can be added in moderation

to salads, soups and stews as a substitute for celery. The dried seeds make a good substitute for celery seed in appropriate recipes.

MINT *(Mentha spp.)*

Mint in the open garden quickly becomes a nuisance, but as a container plant it is both indispensable as a culinary herb and a highly ornamental plant. There are innumerable varieties worthy of inclusion in a herb collection grown in containers, among which are the following:

Apple mint *(Mentha x rotundifolia)*: has pleasant-looking, large, hairy leaves and is often considered to be the finest flavour for cooking, jelly and summer drinks.

Bowles' mint: hybrid, excellent for mint sauce.

Curly mint *(Mentha spicata 'Crispa')*: a form of spearmint with attractively curled, bright green leaves. Used like spearmint.

Ginger mint *(Mentha x gentilis)*: has striking leaves variegated with gold and a faint ginger flavour. Imparts an interesting taste to salads.

PEPPERMINT

(Mentha x pipterata): the characteristic flavour of peppermint is widely recognised. Fresh peppermint is best used in infusions, and sparingly as a decoration for certain cold

puddings and summer sweets.

Red raripila mint *(Mentha x Smithiana 'Rubra')*: good culinary mint with red-tinged leaves.

ROSEMARY *(Rosmarinus sp.)*

Medium-sized or large evergreen shrub which benefits from regular clipping to keep the plant juvenile. This prolongs its life and considerably improved appearance. It is the traditional flavouring for lamb, but can be used with pork and veal. Many ornamental varieties are available. 'Miss Jessup's Variety' has a naturally upright habit, ideal for container growing; 'Severn Sea' is a prostrate form which looks good tumbling over the sides of a container; 'Tuscan Blue' has broader, bright green leaves and bright blue flowers. An interesting, variegated cultivar is also available.

SPEARMINT *(Mentha spicata)*:

the best-known garden mint, which can be used in all recipes calling for fresh mint. Lilac flowers in late summer are subtly attractive and useful as a garnish.

SAGE

Sage is sufficiently well-behaved to be included in mixed herb collections, but is a small shrub that is handsome enough to be grown as

a specimen plant. Common sage *(Salvia officinalis)* has grey-green, slightly woolly leaves and violet, purple, pink or white flowers, and many ornamental-leaved forms are available that are equally useful as a flavouring for goose, duck, pork, veal, sausages and the like. The flavour is strong and the herb should be used sparingly. The following are well worth growing on the patio or balcony:

Golden sage *(Salvia officinalis 'Icterina')*: green and gold variegated leaves and a more compact habit.

Red (purple) sage *(Salvia officinalis 'Purpurescens')*: red leaves and bright blue flowers.

Spanish sage (Salvia lavendulifolia): a small, unusual sage closely resembling lavender, with narrow leaves and early blue flowers. Despite its appearance, it is a true sage and can be used in cooking as such.

Tricoloured sage *(Salvia officinalis 'Tricolor')*: a small, often short-lived sage with grey-green leaves delightfully variegated creamy-white suffused pink and purple.

White sage *(Salvia officinalis 'Albiflora')*: an upright, narrow-leaved form with outstanding white flowers.

SWEET CICELY

(Myrrhis odorata)
Medium-sized perennial herb,

related to angelica, chervil, dill, fennel, lovage, etc., and growing to 1m (39in) in height, with beautiful, long, fern-like leaves and showy heads of pure white flowers in May and June. It can be used like angelica to reduce the acidity of certain tart fruits like rhubarb and gooseberries during cooking, the resultant stewed fruit tastes strongly of aniseed. Chopped leaves may be used in salads and sprinkled over puddings. Surplus roots may be cooked as a vegetable.

TARRAGON
(Artemisia dracunculus)
A herbaceous perennial that spreads in the same way as mint and can become invasive, but is very successful if individually pot-grown. French tarragon is the cook's herb; the Russian form has little taste. Used in fish and chicken dishes, in flavoured vinegars and in omelettes and salads; tarragon butter is served with steaks.

TREE ONION
(Allium cepa var. proliferum)
A perennial onion that forms little bulbs on top of stout hollow stems. These are very hot and can be used sparingly in dishes calling for onion flavour, or pickled.

WINTER SAVORY *(Satureja montana)*
Erect sub-shrub reaching a height of up to 40cm (16in) with narrow, pointed leaves and pale purple or purple-blue flowers. The fresh leaves are added to salads, egg dishes and cooked broad beans. Creeping savory *(Satureja spicigera)* is a smaller, white-flowered species with a creeping habit making it suitable for trough cultivation. It is used in a similar way.

AROMATIC HERBS FOR PLANTING IN PAVING, GRAVEL AND CREVICES

CORSICAN MINT
(Mentha requinii)
A creeping mint with tiny, round leaves and a distinct peppermint smell. Thrives in moist shade and is useful for planting between joints of sunless paving.

CREEPING WILD THYME
(Thymus serpyllum)

PENNYROYAL *(Mentha pulegium)*
A slightly larger, prostrate mint with a good mint fragrance. Must not be eaten as the volatile oils it contains are toxic.

ROMAN OR LAWN CHAMOMILE *(Anthemis nobilis var. 'Treneague')*
A non-flowering form of this

evergreen, perennial herb, with strongly aromatic foliage when walked on.

AROMATIC, SHRUBBY, EVERGREEN HERBS FOR PATIO DECORATION AND FRAGRANCE

ARTEMESIA 'POWIS CASTLE'
Non-flowering, compact sub-shrub with strongly fragrant, finely cut grey leaves.

COTTON LAVENDER
Santolina
Dwarf, mound-forming sub-shrubs with grey, green or silver finely divided foliage and button-like, yellow flowers in summer.

CURRY PLANT
(Helichrysum angustifolium)
Narrow silvery leaves that smell deliciously of curry, and yellow flower heads in summer. It should not be used in cooking as a curry substitute as it is mildly poisonous.

JERUSALEM SAGE
(Phlomis fruticosa)
Grey-green, subtly aromatic, sage-like leaves with eye-catching whorls of sulphur-yellow flowers in late summer and autumn.

LAVENDER
See page 170

ROSEMARY
See page 171

RUSSIAN SAGE
Perowskia 'Blue Spire'
Deeply cut green-grey leaves and large, long, narrow heads of violet-blue flowers in late summer and early autumn.

COTTON LAVENDER
Santolina
Dwarf, mound-forming sub-shrubs with grey, green or silver finely divided foliage and button-like, yellow flowers in summer.

SWEET BAY
See page 169

CULINARY HERBS SUITABLE FOR MIXED PLANTING IN TUBS, TROUGHS, WINDOW BOXES, HANGING POTS AND BASKETS

BASIL (Ocimum basilicum)
A tender perennial with a distinct, clove-like flavour. Use (sparingly) in Italian cookery, tomato dishes, and for flavour-ing salads, soups, minced beef and eggs. Many varieties available, all with slightly different flavours.
Basil 'Minette': dwarf form with characteristic, strong flavour.
Basil 'Red Rubin': purple leaves, attractive salad ingredient.
Basil 'Siam Queen': Another good basil for Thai stir-fries.
Cinnamon basil: cinnamon flavour, ideal for barbecues.
Lemon basil: lemon flavour, excellent with fish.
Lettuce-leaved basil: large leaves, good for salads.
Sweet Basil: large leaves and strong, clove-like fragrance.
Thai basil: red tipped leaves, used in oriental dishes, especially Thai stir-fries.

BERGAMOT
(Monarda didyma)
Aromatic-leaved herbaceous perennial with showy white, pink or red flowers. Orange-tasting leaves can be used in salads and the flowers as a decoration for sweets and puddings.

BORAGE (Borago officinalis)
Annual of medium height with coarsely-hairy leaves and blue flowers. Leaves taste of cucumber and can be added to salads and sandwiches; the edible flowers are used for garnish and as decoration for summer drinks.

CHIVES (Allium tuberosum)
Leaves like grassy onions used to give mild onion flavour to a wide variety of hot, cold, raw and cooked dishes. Mauve flowers used as garnish and decoration. Garlic chives have a mild garlic flavour and are used in a similar way.

ENGLISH MACE
(Achillea decolorans)
Herbaceous perennial with white, flat heads of daisy-like flowers. Aromatic leaves are used in salads and to flavour soups and stews as a substitute for true mace.

FEVERFEW
(Tenacetum)
Ornamental, short-lived perennial with single, white, daisy-like flowers or all-white double ones. The golden-leaved variety 'Aureum' is particularly attractive. The pungent leaves are sometimes chopped and added very sparingly to salads and sandwiches as a control for headaches and migraine.

LEMON BALM
(Melissa officinalis)
Herbaceous perennial growing to about 90cm (3ft) if left to its own devices. It is more attractive when cut back regularly throughout the summer to encourage the production of leaves, which smell strongly of lemon and can be

added freshly chopped to salads, fish dishes and some sweets, or dried and mixed with stuffing ingredients for a lemon flavour. The ornamental forms 'Variegata' and 'Aurea' are especially useful for mixed plantings.

MARJORAM/OREGANO
(Oreganum spp.)
There are three main species of this herb, all of which are used for flavouring meat and poultry, soups and Italian dishes:
Pot marjoram *(Oreganum onites)*: an easily-grown dwarf shrub with some attractive ornamental cultivars, such as the golden leaved 'Aureum' and several fine cream and gold variegated forms.
Sweet marjoram *(Oreganum majorana)* A half-hardy annual. Its flavour is considered by some to be superior to other culinary marjoram forms.
Wild Marjoram or oregano *(Oregano vulgare)*: a low-growing, herbaceous perennial. The leaves dry well and can be stored in a cool, dark place for winter use when the plant itself has died down.

PARSLEY
(Petroselinum crispum)
Popular biennial herb with a wide range of uses. Plain-leaved forms have the best

flavour, curly-leaved varieties are the most decorative. Many named cultivars are available as seed, such as 'Afro', 'Curlina' and 'Moss Curled'. Hamburg parsley *(Petroselinum crispum)* 'Tuberosum' is grown for its edible roots, which can either be grated raw in salads, or cooked as a hot vegetable.

PINEAPPLE MINT *(Mentha suaveolens 'Variegata')*
Woolly mint with cream variegated, grey-green leaves. Young tips used to decorate salads. The unique flavour makes it unsuitable for most mint applications.

PURSLANE
(Portulaca oleracea)
A trailing, annual herb with a clean, sharp taste. A useful addition to salads, or can be cooked as a vegetable.

SALAD BURNET
(Sanguisorba minor)
See leaf salad plants page 166

THYME *(Thymus spp.)*
Low-growing, evergreen shrub, used either mixed with parsley or on its own to flavour meat dishes, soups, stews, fish dishes and stuffings. Many ornamental forms are available.
Thymus serpyllum (wild or creeping thyme): prostrate

habit and a strong, characteristic smell. Many named cultivars are obtainable.
Golden lemon thyme *(Thymus x citriodorus 'Bertram Anderson')*: semi-prostrate variety with bright yellow leaves.
Thymus 'Doone Valley': dwarf, golden variegated thyme with a lemon fragrance.
Thymus 'Porlock': compact, well-shaped bush with dark leaves and an excellent flavour.
Thymus 'Silver Posie': silver-variegated type of lemon-scented thyme.
Thymus doerfleri: long, grey leaves. There are many good named varieties.
Thymus herba-barona:: lemon-scented leaves.
Thymus pseudo-lanuginosus: low-growing form with greyish, woolly leaves.

PLANTS FOR WINDOW SILL CULTIVATION IN THE HOME

CHERVIL, CORIANDER CUMIN, DILL
 APPLE MINT
TARRAGON, BASIL
CHIVES
SWEET MARJORAM, PARSLEY

LEMON GRASS
(Cymbopogon citratus)
A grass-like herb that has

become increasingly popular in recent years with the upsurge in interest in Indian and oriental cookery.

PLANTS WITH EDIBLE DECORATIVE FLOWERS OR PETALS

BERGAMOT
BORAGE
CHIVES
LAVENDER
NASTURTIUM *(Tropaeolum majus vars.)*

POT MARIGOLD (Calendula)
Many ornamental varieties available. Petals and whole heads used in salads, cold soups, etc. Dried petals can be used as a substitute for saffron for colouring food.

ROSES

Strictly speaking, roses are not herbs, but the petals of many have a sweet, subtle flavour. One of the best for culinary purposes is *Rosa gallica* 'Officinalis' (the Apothecary's rose) which grows about 1m (39in) tall and has strongly scented, semi-double, magenta flowers, the petals of which can be crystallised, or used to flavour confectionery, rose honey, rose vinegar. Many other roses, especially those with deep red, heavily scent-

ed flowers, may be used in a similar way.

SWEET ROCKET

(Hesperis matronalis)
A biennial or short-lived perennial, with white, pink, mauve or purple fragrant flowers throughout summer. Delicate petals add interest to cold sweets.

WILD PANSY, HEARTSEASE

(Viola tricolor)
Dainty flowers will brighten up summer cold dishes. Flowers can be crystallised in a similar way to sweet violets. Flowers have a distinctive, fragrant flavour. Leaves are hot and spicy and are useful for adding interest to salads. Many named varieties are available.

APPENDIX 3
Suitable fruit for restricted areas

BUSH FRUIT SUITABLE FOR CONTAINERS OR TRAINING

BLACKCURRANTS
'Ben Connan': early, compact habit, heavy cropper. Pest and disease resistant
'Ben Lomond': compact, late fruiting variety with large, sweet berries.
'Ben More': similar to 'Ben Lomond', but habit is neater and fruit more acid.
'Ben Nevis': similar to 'Ben Lomond', but habit is more upright.
'Ben Sarek': dwarf bushes very suited to container growing.

RED CURRANTS
'Jonkheer van Tets': early, bright red, juicy fruit. Trains well as a cordon. 'Laxton's No 1' is similar.
'Junifer': new, high-yielding, early variety, cropping on new and old wood.
'Stanza': Compact bushes. Small, dark red, acid fruit.

WHITE CURRANTS
'Blanka': Large, excellently-flavoured berries on long trusses in August.
'White Versailles': very popular early variety producing long

trusses of pearly, translucent berries.

GOOSEBERRIES
'Fireball': high-yielding, disease resistant, dessert/culinary variety with large red berries
'Greenfinch': compact, erect bushes. Green fruits with good flavour.
'Jubilee': compact, disease-resistant variety, fruiting early and producing large crops of well-flavoured berries.
'Golden Drop': good, yellow-skinned dessert variety. Neat habit.
'Lord Derby': compact bush with attractive, pendulous shape. Smooth, very dark fruit.
'May Duke': compact bushes. Fruit is red when ripe.
'Pax': almost spineless bushes with red, tasty, decorative fruit.
'Rokula': full-flavoured, red gooseberry with good disease resistance.
'Rolonda': giant, sweet gooseberry suitable for training as standard or cordon.
'Whitesmith': heavy-cropping, culinary and dessert variety that trains very well.

CANE FRUIT

BLACKBERRIES AND HYBRID BERRIES FOR SCREENS AND WALLS
Blackberries
THORNED VARIETIES
'Ashton Cross': August–November. Wiry stems and heavy crops with true blackberry flavour.
'Fantasia': new variety with pleasant flavour and extremely large barries.

THORNLESS VARIETIES
'Adrienne': late July–late August. Shiny, well-flavoured berries.
'Black Satin': vigorous, decorative variety suitable for arch or pergola.
'Helen': early. Attractive, arching habit. Good flavour.
'Loch Ness': August–September. Neat, upright habit requiring little support. Heavy crop of sweet berries.
'Merton Thornless': August–September. Short canes and pleasant flavour.
'Oregon Thornless': September–October. Decorative, semi-evergreen, parsley-like foliage.
'Waldo': very early (July),

exceptionally compact habit. Large, shiny berries.

Hybrid berries

Boysenberry (loganberry x blackberry x raspberry): July–August. Fruit resembles a large, purple-red raspberry with a blackberry flavour. Thornless boysenberry: a thornless, less vigorous variety of the above.

Hildaberry (boysenberry x tayberry): June–July. Large, ornamental flowers and heavy crops of rounded berries.

Japanese wineberry (*Rubus phoenicolasus*): August. Red or orange fruit and ornamental canes covered in bright red bristles.

Loganberry (raspberry x blackberry) LY59: mid-July–August Long, dark red, acid fruit.

LY654 Similar to above, but thornless.

Marionberry: mid-July–September A blackberry with a loganberry-like flavour.

Silvanberry: early August–September. Large, sweet fruit. Vigorous habit makes it only suitable for large pergolas and screens.

Sunberry (raspberry x blackberry): long cropping period from mid-July. Loganberry-like flavour. Vigorous.

Tayberry (blackberry x raspberry): mid-July–August. Large, sweet, purple-red fruits

are ideal for both dessert and culinary use. Preferably choose 'Medana' form, which is virus-free.

Tummelberry (tayberry x tayberry seedling): mid-July–August. Upright habit. Fruit with a flavour similar to tayberry but sharper.

Youngberry (Loganberry x dewberry): late July–September. Fruit like a compact loganberry, juicy with few seeds. Thornless youngberry is similar but canes are smooth.

RASPBERRIES WITH A LONG CROPPING SEASON FOR SCREENING

'Allgold' ('Fallgold'): August–October. Sweet, yellow fruit on current season's canes.

'Autumn Bliss': August–October. Large, red fruit on current season's canes.

'Glen Garry': early July–mid-August. Large, pale red, well-flavoured berries.

'Glen Magna': very large, sweet, firm fruit, good for freezing.

'Glen Moy': late June–late August. Large, sweet berries.

'Glen Prossen': early July–mid-August. Firm, red berries, good for freezing.

'Glen Rosa': early July–late August. Bright red fruit with good shelf life.

'Glen Shee': early July–late

August. High yields of attractive, firm, red fruits with excellent flavour.

'Joy': mid-July–late August. Good yields of superior flavour.

'Leo': fruits August to frost. Large, firm, aromatic berries.

'Zeva': fruits August to frost. Large, good flavoured berries. Fruits on current season's canes.

CLIMBING FRUITS

GRAPES
Black dessert outdoor varieties

'Brandt': heavy crops of sweet grapes and decorative foliage with brilliant autumn colour. Grapes also suitable for red or rosé wine.

'Dornfelder': early, red grape with good autumn colouring.

White dessert outdoor varieties

'Madeleine Angevine': heavy-cropping, dual-purpose grape.

'Madeleine Syvaner': early ripening, pale grape that can also be used for wine making.

Wine grapes

'Müller Thürgau': sweet, late-ripening, heavy-yielding white grape.

'Triomphe d'Alsace': strong, heavy cropper producing a red wine of strong flavour.

KIWI FRUIT

Vigorous climbers suitable for pergolas and large walls. Male and female plants are required for pollination. 'Hayward' is the best female; 'Tomuri' a reliable male.

Mini-kiwi 'Issai': a more compact, self-fertile, plant suitable for limited areas. Sweet fruits the size of a large gooseberry. Thin skin should not be removed before peeling.

CONSERVATORY FRUITS FOR CONTAINERS

BANANA

(Musa paradisiaca) Common banana: makes a large, architectural plant bearing full-sized, edible bananas when mature. Too large for most conservatories. A better choice is *Musa acuminata* 'Cavendishii', the dwarf or Canary Island banana, which grows to around 1.8m (6ft) while still producing good-sized fruit.

CITRUS

Lemon *(Citrus limon)*
'Tipo Tuscano': dwarf bush with fragrant white flowers, tinged red. Flowers and small fruits produced throughout the year.
'Meyer': medium-sized fruits with crisp, juicy flesh.
'Ponderosa': huge, yellow-orange fruits with thick, rough skins

Orange

(Citrus auranticum) Seville orange: spiny bush producing round, orange, rough-skinned fruit used in marmalade making.

Citrus limonia (C. taitensis or C. otaitensis) Otaheite orange: a hybrid between the lemon and the mandarin orange. Small, thornless shrub with purple-tinged, white flowers and rounded deep yellow or orange fruits up to 5cm (2in) in diameter.

Citrus mitis (Citrofortunella mitis) Calamondin orange: a small, thornless bush bearing many flowers and miniature, bitter oranges at the same time from an early age. The fruits are suitable for marmalade making. The variegated form is particularly ornamental.

Citrus reticulata Mandarin orange: small bush when container-grown producing rounded orange fruits with a characteristic flavour.

Citrus sinensis (sweet orange): spiny shrub growing to about 1.2m (4ft) when restrained in a pot, with sweet-tasting, bright orange fruit up to 8cm (3in) across. Several named varieties available.

Other members of the citrus family, such as varieties of lime and grapefruit suitable for home conservatory cultivation, are also available from specialist nurseries and plant importers. Citrus can also be easily grown from pips; the resultant plants are attractive but the fruit is unpredictable.

GRAPES

'Buckland Sweetwater': compact vine bearing round, sweet grapes that turn from pale green to golden yellow on ripening.

'Foster's Seedling': possibly the best white 'Sweetwater', with very large bunches of very sweet fruit.

'Black Hamburg': popular, easily grown black vine with big, black juicy grapes.

KUMQUAT

(Fortunella margarita)
A small bush resembling, though not actually related to, citrus, bearing scented white flowers followed by oval fruit 4cm (around 2in) long which are eaten whole without peeling. Generally used for garnishing or pickled in brandy. An ornamental variegated form is available.

OLIVE

(Olea europaea)
A novelty sometimes available by mail order and can be found in many nurseries. Produces edible, normal-sized olives and will withstand hot summer sun and a position near a central heating radiator in winter.

POMEGRANATE

(Punica granatum) 'Nana'
Dwarf pomegranate
Bushy plant to about 90cm
(3ft) in height with glossy
leaves and bright scarlet
flowers. Dwarf, ball-like fruits
that are edible but full of
seeds.

FIG

'Bourjasotte Grise': a green,
tender fig which does well
when pot-grown, producing
sweet, round figs with a rich,
delicious flavour.

MELONS

'Exclusive F1': early, large fruit
with pale green flesh and a
delicious aroma and flavour.
'Ogen': a 'Sweetheart'-type
melon suitable where some
heat is available.
'Sweetheart F1': attractive,
sweet succulent flesh.

PASSION FRUIT

(Passiflora edulis) Purple
granadilla: An interesting fruit
with a leathery, purple skin
and orange-yellow flesh with
a distinctive fragrance and
taste.
Passiflora quadrangularis
Sweet granadilla: attractive,
fragrant flowers of typical,
'passion flower' formation
and large, showy, orange, oval
fruits that are sweet and tasty.

CONSERVATORY FRUIT FROM PIPS, SEEDS AND STONES

Many shop-bought fruit
contain seeds that can be
easily germinated in the
home. Most produce attractive plants that can be used
for indoor decoration, though
many species will form very
large specimens before
reaching maturity. Any fruit,
unfortunately, is usually
unpredictable, either regarding quality or the length of
time taken to form, and high
light levels are usually necessary. It can be fun to experiment, however.

HEATHLAND BERRIES

BLUEBERRIES
Cranberry
Popular, large, red fruits produced in July. Cultivate as
blueberries.
Highbush blueberries
'Blue Crop','Earliblue',
'Goldtraube','Herbert','Jersey',
'Patriot': pink and white flowers followed by blue berries
with a grey bloom. Plant in
water-retentive, lime-free
compost. Two varieties are
needed for good pollination.
Lowbush blueberry
(whortleberry, bilberry, blae-
berry): blackish berries with
grey-blue bloom. Cultivated
like highbush blueberries.

RHUBARB

NB Rhubarb is technically a
vegetable but is generally considered to be a dessert crop.
Varieties with ornamental
stems suitable for tub
cultivation
'Caywood Delight': ruby
coloured stems that retain
shape and colour when
cooked. Excellent flavour.
'Timperley Early': a naturally
early variety which can be
forced under a bucket in late
winter.
'Victoria': bright red, low acid
stems.

SOFT FRUITS

STRAWBERRIES
Alpine and decorative strawberries for edgings and ornamental areas
'Alexandria': large, juicy fruits.
No runners.
'Baron Solemacher': huge
crops of tiny, sweet-flavoured
berries. Can be planted in partial shade. No runners.
'Cezan': seed-raised strawberry fruiting in its first season.
Often sold as plug plants with
ornamental summer bedding
species in spring.
'Fragaria Pink Panda': a herbaceous perennial of the strawberry family with pink flowers
and edible fruit. 'Red Ruby' is
similar but with red flowers.
Produces many runners.
'Serenata': another strawberry-

type plant with attractive shiny leaves, pink flowers and alpine-type fruits. Produces many runners.

STRAW BERRIES FOR HANGING BASKETS AND OTHER CONTAINERS

Best of the earlies
'Emily': will crop in May if grown under cloches or in a cold frame or conservatory.
'Gigantella Maxim': June–August. Huge, well-shaped fruit.
'Honeoye': fruits from early June. Attractive fruits, heavy crops, disease resistant.
'Senga Gigana': late June–July. Massive crops of large fruit.

Perpetual and repeat-fruiting varieties
'Aromel': crops June-July and August–September. Large fruit, excellent flavour. Tumbling habit.
'Bolero': June-September. Firm, glossy, orange-red fruits with good flavour.
'Calypso': firm, glossy berries.
'Evita': July–October. High yielding, firm fruit.
'Florence': July–mid-August. Firm, well-shaped fruit with true strawberry flavour.
'Guirlande': long cropping season from late June. Very heavy crops of large, sweet fruit. Long runners and cascading habit.
'Mount Kenya': produces exceptionally long runners

that can be trained up a trellis, fence or canes to produce 'climbing' strawberries.
'Ostara': June–September. Large fruits, heavy cropping.
'Pegasus': late June–August. Firm, glossy fruit. Exceptionally high yield.
'Rapella': long cropping season. Heavy crops.
'Senga Sengana': early July–August. Huge crop of dark red strawberries.
'Temptation': a variety specially bred for container planting, with a well-shaped, compact habit and producing fruits throughout the summer.

Pick of the lates
'Auchincruive Climax': an old, heavy cropping variety with attractive fruits and a good flavour.
'Elsanta': late July. Glossy, orange-red fruits, heavy crops.
'Laura': very late, with long picking season. Fine flavour and good cropper.
'Symphony': August. Easy to grow, attractive berries.

TREE FRUITS
APPLES
Apples suitable for grafting onto very dwarfing rootstock (M27) or dwarfing rootstock (M9) for tub cultivation, mini-cordons and cordons, espaliers and fans, dwarf and small family trees and step-overs
Cooking apples
'Annie Elizabeth': golden skin

with red cheeks. Cream flesh.
'Bramley, Clone 20': a less vigorous clone producing heavier crops.
'Howgate Wonder': huge apples, ripe fruit may be eaten raw.

Dessert apples
'Ashmead's Kernel': pale green, tangy flavour.
'Blenheim Orange': orange-yellow skin, sweet. Also cooks well.
'Charles Ross': orange-red flushed skin. Also bakes well.
Self-fertile 'Cox': a clone of this well-known apple requiring no separate pollinator.
'Croquella': naturally dwarf, bushy apple, good for pots.
'Egremont Russet': yellow-skinned russet with nutty flavour.
'Falstaff', 'Red Falstaff': crisp, sweet and juicy.
'Fiesta': yellow, flushed red. Flavour similar to 'Cox's Orange Pippin'.
'Gala': pale green, flecked scarlet. Crisp and juicy.
'Granny Smith': dark green skin, crisp and juicy.
'Greensleeves': green-skinned, sweet and juicy with a hint of honey.
'James Grieve': red and green skins. Juicy, cooks well.
'Jonagold': red and gold fruit with fragrant, sweet flesh.
'Jupiter': orange-red and yellow skin. Juicy.
'Katy': pale yellow, flushed red. Firm, juicy and sweet.

'Kidd's Orange Red': lemon yellow, flushed scarlet. Aromatic flavour.

'Laxton's Superb': easily grown, Cox-like apple.

'Lilliput': naturally small habit. Good flavour, late, excellent in pots.

'Lord Lambourne': heavy cropper, refreshing and sweet.

'Orleans Reinette': golden yellow skin, flushed red, Nutty flavour. Can also be cooked.

'Red Devil': deep red skin and pink, strawberry-flavoured flesh.

'Sunset': another 'Cox'-like apple.

'Winter Gem': pink-flushed fruit, late. 'Cox'-like flavour.

'Worcester Pearmain': scarlet skin, pure white flesh. Strawberry flavour. Early.

Ballerina apple trees for containers and screening

'Bolero': early, green-skinned with gold flush.

'Charlotte': 'Bramley'-like cooker.

'Flamenco': dark red, white flesh. Keeps well.

'Polka': red and green skin. Fairly early.

'Waltz': red and green apple. Late.

'Maypole': ornamental and edible crab apple with carmine flowers, purple young foliage turning green and large, purple 'crabs'.

Compatible apples for family trees and fan-trained family trees

'James Grieve', 'Sunset', 'Winter Gem'

'Discovery', 'Charles Ross', 'James Grieve'

'Fiesta', 'Falstaff', 'Bramley'

'James Grieve', 'Spartan', 'Self-fertile Cox'

'Sunset', 'Egremont Russet', 'James Grieve'

'Gala', 'James Grieve', 'Worcester Pearmain'

'Ellison's Orange', 'Sunset', 'Tydeman's Early Worcester' (early form of 'Worcester Pearmain')

'James Grieve', 'Sunset', 'Worcester Pearmain'

Minarette and pillarette apple trees for containers and screens

Self-fertile 'Cox', 'Discovery', 'Ellisons's Orange', 'Fiesta', 'Howgate Wonder', 'James Grieve', 'Laxton's Superb', 'Red Falstaff', 'Sunset', 'Winter Gem'.

CHERRIES

Self fertile varieties suitable for grafting onto 'Tabel' rootstock for container cultivation and fan-training

'Celeste': naturally dwarf and compact. Dark red, juicy fruits.

'Cherokee': large, sweet fruits with a first-class flavour.

'Compact Stella': compact form of 'Stella' with all the same attributes. Makes a first-rate tub specimen.

'Lapins': very large, dark fruits. Very sweet. Heavy cropper.

'Morello': cooking cherry suitable for a north wall.

'Stella': heavy crops of dark red fruit with an excellent flavour.

'Sunburst': large, red, very sweet cherries.

'Summer Sun': fairly compact habit. Dark red fruits with a silver sheen.

DWARF APRICOT FOR THE PATIO AND BALCONY

'Luizet': very large, early fruit with a true apricot flavour. Reasonably hardy.

FIGS FOR TUB CULTIVATION AND FAN-TRAINING

'Brown Turkey': a reliable, red-fleshed fig producing heavy crops of good-flavoured fruit.

'Brunswick': another dark-fleshed variety ripening slightly earlier than 'Brown Turkey' but with a slightly lower yield.

'White Marseilles': a green fig with white flesh. Excellent for pot cultivation.

NECTARINES

Dwarf nectarine for patio and balcony cultivation

'Nectarella': deep pink, attractive spring blossom. Firm, succulent yellow fruits.

Nectarines for a sunny wall

'Lord Napier': large yellow fruits, flushed red, with a superb flavour.

'Pineapple': greenish-yellow, flushed red. Rich flavour with a hint of pineapple.

PEARS

Compatible pears for family trees and fan-trained family trees
'Williams', 'Conference', 'Doyenne du Comice' 'Concorde', 'Beth', 'Williams' Minarettes and pillarettes suitable for tub cultivation and screening
'Beth', 'Beurre Hardy', 'Concorde', 'Conference', 'Williams Bon Chrétien'.
Varieties suitable for grafting onto Quince C semi-dwarfing rootstock for tub cultivation and for training as espaliers and fans
'Beth': pale yellow skin, soft and juicy, early.
'Beurre Hardy': russet-bronze, white flesh, early.
'Concorde': possibly the best all-round pear. Delicious flavour, large, well-shaped fruit, firm but juicy. Self-fertile. Mid-season.

'Conference': firm, good flavour. Self-fertile but better-shaped fruits with a pollinator. Early.
'Doyenne du Comice': yellow russet with red flush. Early but stores well.
'Moonglow': lemon yellow skin, excellent flavour. Very early.
'Onward': greenish-yellow flushed orange-red and russet. Soft and sweet. Mid-season.
'Williams Bon Chrétien': very early, to enjoy at their best, should be ripened on the tree and eaten immediately.
'Winter Nellis' ('Nelis'): late, good keeper. Fragrant flesh.

PEACHES

'Bonanza': very large fruits heavily flushed red.
'Garden Lady': dwarf peach with masses of ornamental, pink flowers in spring and well-flavoured, golden-fleshed fruits in August.
'Peregrine': a reliable, outdoor peach that grows well in containers and makes an excellent wall-trained subject.
'Ponderosa': small variety with decorative spring blossom and yellow-skinned fruit overlaid bright red.
'Rochester': standard variety that makes a good fan-trained plant for a sunny wall.

PLUMS AND GAGES

Self-fertile varieties suitable for container growing on 'Pixy' semi-dwarfing rootstock and for training as fans on 'St. Julian A' rootstock
'Avalon': large, round fruit with red-yellow skins and golden-yellow flesh. Mid-August.
'Hermon': medium-sized, blue black plums with bloom. Late July.
'Marjorie's Seedling': large, purple, oval plums with yellow flesh. Late September.
'Rivers Early Prolific': abundant crops of small, purple-blue plums. Early August.
'Victoria': most popular dessert plum with deliciously flavoured, pale red fruits. Late August.
'Yellow Pershore': golden yellow fruit. Mid-August.
'Cambridge Gage': small, yellowish-green, sweet fruits. Late August.
'Coe's Golden Drop': medium-sized, amber fruits with lovely, rich flavour. Late September.
'Denniston's Superb': heavy crops of large, green fruit. Late August.
'Early Transparent': apricot-yellow fruits, excellent flavour. August.
'Willingham Gage': very heavy cropper. Mid-August.

APPENDIX 4

Patio kitchen garden sowing and planting timetable

JANUARY

Plant bare-root fruit trees and bushes in containers and as screens and wall plants.

Sow 'windowsill' salad plants indoors.

Plant Jerusalem artichokes and bare-root rhubarb.

FEBRUARY

Plant bare-root fruit trees and bushes in containers and as screens and wall plants.

Plant bare-root strawberry plants in containers and as edgings.

Sow 'windowsill' salad plants indoors.

Plant onion and shallot sets and garlic in pots and trays under glass.

Plant Jerusalem artichokes and bare-root rhubarb.

MARCH

Plant bare-root fruit trees and bushes in containers and as screens and wall plants.

Plant bare-root strawberry plants in containers.

Plant Jerusalem artichokes and bare-root rhubarb.

Sow 'windowsill' salad plants indoors.

Sow early peas and broad beans in pots and modules (cells) indoors.

Plant potatoes in barrels and pots.

Plant onion and shallot sets and garlic in pots and trays.

Sow half-hardy vegetables (tomatoes, peppers, aubergines, cucumbers, courgettes, sweet corn, morelle de balbis, korila, cape gooseberry, tomatillo) in trays and modules indoors.

Sow cardoon and globe artichoke seed indoors.

Sow cabbage, calabrese, cauliflower, broccoli, kale and kohl rabi in seed trays and pots.
Sow hardy vegetables such as lettuce, salad leaf vegetables, onions (seed), carrots, beetroot, turnips, parsnips, spinach, leaf beet, and radish in modules.

APRIL

Continue sowing half-hardy vegetables (tomatoes, peppers, aubergines, cucumbers, courgettes, sweet corn, morelle de balbis, korila, cape gooseberry, tomatillo) in trays and modules indoors. Pot-on seedlings sown earlier.

Plant pot-grown fruit trees and bushes in containers and as screens and wall plants.

Plant pot-grown 'strawberries in containers and as edgings.

Sow 'windowsill' salads indoors.

Continue sowing hardy vegetables such as lettuce, salad leaf vegetables, onions (seed), carrots, beetroot, turnips, parsnips, chard, spinach, leaf beet and radish in modules.

Sow maincrop peas, broad beans, dwarf French beans and runner beans in pots.

Sow cardoon and globe artichoke seed indoors.

Plant potatoes in barrels and pots.

Continue sowing cabbage, calabrese, cauliflower, broccoli, kale and kohl rabi in seed trays.

Plant onion sets, shallots, garlic and early pea and bean plants in growing bags and other containers.

Plant early, module-raised seedlings of lettuce, salad leaf vegetables, onions (seed), carrots, beetroot, turnips, parsnips, chard, spinach, leaf beet and radish in growing bags and other containers.

Sow paracress, dragonhead, orache and strawberry spinach in pots and modules.

MAY

Pot-on remainder of half-hardy vegetable seedlings (tomatoes, peppers, aubergines, cucumbers, courgettes, sweet corn, morelle de balbis, korila, cape gooseberry, tomatillo).

Plant out seedlings of lettuce, salad leaf vegetables, onions (seed), carrots, beetroot, turnips, parsnips, chard, spinach, leaf beet and radish raised in pots and

modules into growing bags and other containers. Plant out cabbage, calabrese, cauliflower, broccoli, kale and kohl rabi seedlings in containers.

Plant pot-grown fruit trees and bushes in containers and as screens and wall plants.

Plant pot-grown strawberries in containers and as edgings.

Sow 'windowsill' salads indoors.

Sow radishes and spring onions for succession.

Plant herbs in containers and in the ground.

Plant potatoes in barrels and pots.

Continue sowing lettuce, salad leaf vegetables, onions (seed), carrots, beetroot, turnips, spinach and radish in modules.

Sow maincrop peas, dwarf French beans and runner beans in pots.

Plant cardoons and globe artichokes in permanent positions.

Plant strawberry spinach, dragonhead, orache and para cress in open ground or containers.

Plant pot-grown rhubarb. Plant pot-raised early peas and broad and French beans in growing bags.

JUNE

Plant out cabbage, cauliflower, broccoli, kale and kohl rabi seedlings in containers.

Plant out seedlings of lettuce, salad leaf vegetables, onions (seed), beetroot, turnips, spinach and radish raised in pots and modules into growing bags and other containers.

Plant pot-grown fruit trees and bushes in containers and as screens and wall plants.

Plant pot-grown strawberries in containers and as edgings.

Plant half-hardy vegetables (tomatoes, peppers, aubergines, cucumbers, courgettes, sweet corn, morelle de balbis, korila, cape gooseberry, tomatillo) outdoors.

Sow 'windowsill' salads indoors
.
Sow spring onions and radishes for succession.

Plant herbs in containers and in the ground.

Plant pot-grown rhubarb.
Plant cardoons and
artichokes in permanent
positions
.
Plant pot-raised maincrop
peas and French and runner
beans in containers.

JULY

Plant pot-grown fruit trees
and bushes in containers
and as screens and wall
plants.

Plant pot-grown
strawberries in containers
and as edgings.

Sow 'windowsill' salads
indoors.

Plant herbs in containers
and in the ground.

Sow radishes and spring
onions for succession.

Plant early potatoes in pots
for Christmas and the New
Year.

Plant pot-grown rhubarb.

AUGUST

Plant pot-grown fruit trees
and bushes in containers
and as screens and wall
plants.

Plant pot-grown
strawberries in containers
and as edgings.

Sow 'windowsill' salads
indoors.

Plant herbs in containers
and in the ground.

Plant early potatoes in pots
for Christmas and the New
Year.

Plant pot-grown rhubarb.

Sow corn salad and land
cress in pots for winter use.

SEPTEMBER

Plant pot-grown fruit trees
and bushes in containers
and as screens and wall
plants.

Plant pot-grown
strawberries in containers
and as edgings.

Sow 'windowsill' salads
indoors.

Plant herbs in containers
and in the ground.

Plant pot-grown rhubarb.
Sow corn salad and land
cress in pots for winter use.

OCTOBER

Plant pot-grown fruit trees
and bushes in containers
and as screens and wall
plants.

Plant pot-grown
strawberries in containers
and as edgings.

Sow 'windowsill' salads
indoors.

NOVEMBER

Plant pot-grown and bare-
root fruit trees and bushes in
containers and as screens
and wall plants.

Plant bare-root strawberries
in containers and as
edgings.

Sow 'windowsill' salads
indoors.

Plant Jerusalem artichokes
and rhubarb crowns.

DECEMBER

Plant pot-grown and bare-
root fruit trees and bushes in
containers and as screens
and wall plants.

Plant bare-root
strawberries in containers
and as edgings.

Sow 'windowsill' salads
indoors.

Plant Jerusalem artichokes
and rhubarb crowns.

Index